The Pure Joy of
Monastery Cooking

The Pure Joy of Monastery Cooking

Essential Meatless Recipes for the Home Cook

Brother Victor-Antoine d'Avila-Latourrette

THE COUNTRYMAN PRESS · WOODSTOCK, VT.

Cover photos by Mick Hales
Cover and interior design by Liz Trovato

Interior photographs by Mick Hales (except as noted below)

iStock photographs pages: 19 (mcfields), 23 (Matejay), 24 (Milacroft), 28 (kjohansen), 29 (bravajulia), 31 (Ca2hill), 36 (YinYang), 37 (ac_bnphotos), 39 (dyoma), 42 (sunara), 47 (kcline), 63 (knape), 70 (AbbieImages), 74 (peolsen), 78 (fstop123), 79 (douglascraig), 88 (Creativeye99), 89 (jojobob), 93 (parema), 94 (Frantab), 95 (Professor25), 100 (Funwithfood), 101 (ChrisAt), 103 (RawFile), 109 (robynmac), 111 (JohnnyGreig), 114 (stevemccallum), 117 (ason), 119 (flugga), 120 (R0b), 121 (robynmac), 126 (Victorburnside), 127 (Angelika), 129 (Chiyacat), 133 (adlifemarketing), 136 (riakhel), 140 (Stieglitz), 145 (PeterJSeager), 147 (BruceBlock), 151 (brytta), 152 (GomezDavid), 153 (Stieglitz), 155 (JohnPeacock), 158 (GomezDavid), 161 (piccerella), 164 (jeffrauch), 168 (salsachica), 173 (Elenathewise), 174 (gaffera), 179 (fotoflare), 189 (KevinDyer), 196 (tilo), 197 (MonaMakela), 199 (Ockra), 201 (Elenathewise), 202 (Issaurinko), 206 (Smitt), 213 (kcline), 215 (shank_ali), 219 (kcline), 228 (eliane), 231 (Tschon), 236 (ugurbariskan), 237 (RoderickMacte), 238 (ivanmateev), 241 (dirkr), 248 (CW03070), 250 (YuriyS), 256 (vm), 258 (kkgas), 259 (SasPartout)

Charles Clough photographs pages: 13, 49, 60, 64, 66, 83, 122, 150, 162, 165, 234, 236, 265, 268

Produced by Print Matters, Inc., www.printmattersinc.com

Published by The Countryman Press
P.O. Box 748
Woodstock, VT 05091
Distributed by W. W. Norton & Company, Inc.
500 Fifth Avenue
New York, NY 10110

Printed in China

The Pure Joy of Monastery Cooking
ISBN 978-0-88150-922-9

10 9 8 7 6 5 4 3 2 1

Dedication

*The monks should wait on one another. No one is to be
excused from kitchen service, unless he is ill or engaged in
another important task . . . Let the monks serve each other
in charity.*

—Rule of St. Benedict, *chapter 35*

To countless generations of monks and nuns who, in true
Gospel spirit, have performed the humble labor of kitchen
service for their brothers and sisters in the Lord, and who
are my inspiration in the garden and kitchen. Deo gratias!

Acknowledgments

I wish to thank all those who closely collaborated in bringing out this new book: Kermit Hummel and Lisa Sacks of
The Countryman Press; my producer, Richard Rothschild of
Print Matters; and Jennifer Lyons of the Jennifer Lyons
Literary Agency. Michael Hales for his extraordinary sen-
sitivity to monastic photography. Kathy Herald Marlowe
and Michael Marlowe for the generous use of their beautiful kitchen. Michael Centore, who patiently worked many of
the book's details. And the student interns from Vassar
College who help at the monastery with typing and a great
many other tasks. My sincere gratitude to all.

Contents

Introduction, page 11

PART THREE
Side Dishes

PART FOUR
Meal Accents

PART FIVE
Final Course

Index, page 261

Introduction

 few years ago, when I wrote *From a Monastery Kitchen*, a small collection of vegetarian recipes composed in our own small monastery kitchen, I was surprised to see how many people embraced my book with its message of health-oriented cuisine. The book sold well over a million copies worldwide with editions in French, Italian, German, Dutch, and Japanese, among other languages. It even won first prize in the annual international cookbook competition in Paris.

The success of that book has much to do with the evolution that has occurred in our eating habits during the last few decades. Vegetarian fare is no longer looked down upon as the domain of a few health fanatics. Our eating habits have evolved so much in recent years that, today, many people around the world embrace a virtually meat-free diet without considering themselves to be pure or strict vegetarians. Some adopt this sort of diet for philosophical or religious reasons; others, perhaps the majority, do it for reasons of health and economics. There is no doubt in my mind that a basic vegetarian diet, such as the monastic one, embraces and intertwines in its own simplicity both principles: healthy eating and the economic restraints of many in our world today. There is nothing wrong in thinking and trying to live by the principle that some of us may decide to consume less so that those who have less may be able to consume more.

This interest in all sorts of food and cooking and the continual discovery and infinite ranges of nonmeat dishes from all corners of the world continue to fascinate people across the country. Nowadays, prestigious and ordinary restaurants alike make available to their customers an endless variety of dishes based on vegetables, grains, nuts, fruits, eggs, and cheese that was unthinkable only a few decades ago. Our understanding of food and the preference for a healthy diet have evolved to such a point that we now have the luxury of choosing from among some of the most innovative, exciting, and delicious dishes that emerged from the conception of a health-based cuisine. Our own appreciation for good and more intricate food has also increased. The choice of a basic nonmeat diet is not only for health nuts, as it was once considered to be; it is for everyone, for people of all ages and lifestyles, including those who may still occasionally eat meat. The decision to relinquish meat altogether is a very personal one, one that's done gradually, thoughtfully, after arriving at a certain point in our lives where we can assert for ourselves the adoption of a well-balanced vegetarian diet. And sometimes it takes time and experimentation to acquire that balance.

Throughout the years, I have received many letters from home cooks around the world, thanking me for producing simple recipes that allowed them to discover the joys of a healthier diet. As people gain confidence and trust in this sort of cuisine, they begin to experiment, discovering a variety of flavors, textures, aromas, and colors they had not known before. It becomes for many the true art of *dégustation*, as the French love to call it.

I use the term *vegetarian* in a loose way here. I am well aware of the endless gamut of vegetarians or semivegetarians in the world. There are many degrees of vegetarianism. Some include eggs and cheese in their diets (as most monasteries do). Others partake of fish and chicken but not of red meat. And there are others who, for one reason or another, may include an occasional meat dish in their diets. Vegans exclude all animal products, including milk, cheese, yogurt, and eggs, from their diets. Personally, I prefer a diet that includes eggs and dairy products, for they often offer the sort of protein we need to keep a balanced diet.

This book is arranged in five parts by type of food preparation and the place they occupy in the context of a civilized meal:

- Part 1 consists of food or plates assembled to introduce a meal: hors d'oeuvres, appetizers, and soups.
- Part 2 consists of dishes that could be presented as the main course: egg dishes, crêpes and pancakes, casseroles, grains, rice, pasta, couscous, etc.
- Part 3 presents what could be considered side dishes or accompaniments to the main course (Italians call them *contorni*): vegetables and mushrooms.
- Part 4 consists of what I call "meal accents," for lack of a better term; these include salads, sauces, and breads.
- Part 5 focuses on the final course: fruit and dessert.

This is neither a diet book nor a health food book, per se. On the contrary, while accepting and adhering to the basic principle of a health-oriented diet, the book is designed to expand the horizons of that particular type of nutrition.

These recipes show the endless possibilities available to those who wholeheartedly embrace this sort of cuisine. One can remain a humble vegetarian yet also be a grand connoisseur of the art of cooking, of a refined cuisine that places the accent on good, healthy, tasty food for its own sake. The ample variety of recipes presented is clear proof that one can cultivate a healthy lifestyle while also enjoying all the basic pleasures of the table. Moreover, these recipes offer a broad culinary repertoire that can please the most refined of palates. They also make available to all—vegetarians and nonvegetarians alike—delicious, honest food from all over the world.

The systematic order and presentation of the recipes allows and may inspire the cook to prepare a well-constructed menu, a menu that can be both appetizing to the senses and intelligent and wise to the mind. There is nothing more rewarding or civilized than a well-planned meal. When it happens, it is an occasion for celebration and pure joy.

The *The* Pure Joy *of* Monastery Cooking

Part One

Introduction to the Meal

*Hors d'oeuvres, Appetizers,
and Soups*

Hors d'oeuvres and Appetizers

In France, where the traditional hors d'oeuvres originated, they are considered very much a state of mind. These lovely appetizers—be they Spanish tapas, Italian antipasti, French hors d'oeuvres, or some other starter—always seem to anticipate the joys of a good meal to come, creating among those who nibble on them a spirit of conviviality, friendship, and camaraderie. These delicious little bites serve well the purposes of stimulating the appetite yet calming down people's hunger while they wait patiently for the meal to be served.

A good appetizer, no matter how simple it may be, when well prepared and well presented is often portrayed as an exquisite work of art. Appetizers, after all, are not an everyday event; they are usually created for special celebratory meals or occasional evenings of fine entertainment. Birthdays, anniversaries, Thanksgiving, Christmas, New Year, Easter, and so on, are all good occasions for anticipating a good meal together, by first delighting ourselves with the rituals of savory appetizers, usually accompanied by a good aperitif or special drink—in France, a glass of Champagne, or a fine chilled Alsatian wine, a Muscadet or other similar, are often served to accompany these hors d'oeuvres. This premeal ritual not only gives a hint of the culinary joys to come, it also creates an ambiance of unique warmth and coziness among the invited. Appetizers, no matter how they are prepared or served, are completely bound by the concept of anticipation and conviviality among those ready to partake of one and the same meal. It is important to keep this in mind when planning a menu that includes appetizers and hors d'oeuvres. These "finger foods," as many call them today, are meant to be light and small in shape and size, for in no way are they intended as a substitute for the real meal. It is also wise to measure or limit the quantity of appetizers served before the meal so that guests are not tempted to fill themselves to capacity before the repast, leaving thus very little space for the food to come.

Among this collection of recipes here described, I include some of my favorite hors d'oeuvres and appetizers. I suggest the reader experiment with them and even modify some of the ingredients, according to his or her own inclination or talents. Sometimes adding a local or seasonal product ends up giving that special personal touch to the recipe. It also is wise to accommodate the tastes of others invited for the occasion—to take the care to learn ahead of time which ingredients are pleasant to one's guests and what foods must be avoided (for example, certain items to which some people may have real allergies or a dislike). Throughout the years, I have been circumspect when I have been told anecdotes about people who ended up terribly sick after consuming some tasteful and delightful canapé before the meal. What a pity and what a fiasco! It is the task of a good cook to always be on the alert—while preparing any food, be it a simple appetizer or an elegant main course, he or she must take into consideration everything that's beneficial to the health and well-being of those invited to his or her table.

Today antipasti have a more formal role. They are served to prepare the palate for the meal that follows, usually accompanied by a chilled glass of Prosecco in the north or spritzy, often homemade, red wine in the south . . . Antipasti memories are legion too, though one of my favorites remains the selection I ate on a farm in the mountains of Basilicata when, at the end of the day, I sat with the farm family around a table and ate aromatic home-cured olives, home-pickled vegetables, homemade sausages, a sumptuous egg and pepper dish, and crostini topped with herbed beans, all washed down with liters of homemade wine.

—Susan Herrmann Loomis, *Italian Farmhouse Cookbook*

Sautéed Peppers with Raisins and Arugula

Makes 8 servings

¹/₄ cup olive oil

2 red bell peppers, cut into ¹/₄-inch strips

2 yellow bell peppers, cut into ¹/₄-inch strips

2 orange bell peppers, cut into ¹/₄-inch strips

¹/₄ cup raisins

4 tablespoons chopped fresh parsley

2 tablespoons balsamic vinegar

Salt and freshly ground pepper

8 cups arugula, whole leaves, plus additional
  for garnish

1 Heat the oil in a very large, heavy skillet over medium-high heat. Add all the peppers; sauté until slightly softened, stirring occasionally, about 7 minutes. Add the raisins and parsley. Continue to cook until the peppers are soft, about 5 minutes. Stir in the vinegar. Season with salt and pepper.

2 Add the arugula to the peppers and stir until the arugula begins to wilt, about 1 minute. Transfer the mixture to a large platter, garnish with the additional arugula, and serve.

Asparagus
Canapés

Makes about 24 canapés

5 tablespoons butter

1/3 cup finely chopped fresh parsley

Salt and freshly ground pepper

6 slices whole wheat bread, cut into four
    squares (each the size of a cracker)

12–14 asparagus stalks, cooked until tender
    and cut into 1-inch lengths

2 ounces grated mozzarella or Gruyère cheese

1 Preheat the oven to 250°F and butter a cookie sheet.

2 Place the butter in a bowl and cream it with the help of a fork. Add the chopped parsley and salt and pepper to taste, and mix well until a creamy, even consistency is achieved.

3 Spread each bread slice evenly with the butter mixture. Place the bread slices in one layer, butter side up, on the prepared cookie sheet.

4 Arrange the asparagus pieces on the bread and sprinkle the grated cheese on top of the asparagus. Place the cookie sheet in the oven and heat for 6–8 minutes, until the cheese melts. Serve hot.

Leeks Vinaigrette

1 Trim the leeks, removing tough outer leaves and all but about 4 inches of the green part. Starting about 1 inch above the root end, slice the leeks in half lengthwise. Open the leeks like a book and wash well in cold running water to remove all sand and dirt. Set aside.

2 Bring salted water to a boil in a large, deep skillet, lay the leeks in the water, and simmer over medium heat until soft, about 7 minutes. Transfer the leeks to a large bowl of cold water to stop them from cooking further. Carefully split the leeks completely in half lengthwise, transfer to a rack, and drain thoroughly.

3 Whisk the mustard, vinegar, and salt and pepper to taste together in a small bowl. Gradually add the oil, whisking constantly, until the vinaigrette is smooth and creamy. Adjust the seasonings and set aside. Remove the leaves from four of the parsley sprigs, chop, and set aside.

4 Divide the leek halves equally among four warm salad plates, arranging them in circles. Drizzle the vinaigrette over the leeks and sprinkle with the chopped parsley. Use the remaining two sprigs as garnish.

Makes 4 servings

8 medium leeks

2 teaspoons Dijon mustard

5 tablespoons red wine vinegar

Sea salt and freshly ground white pepper

7 tablespoons olive oil

6 sprigs parsley

Canapés à la Provençale

Makes 20 canapés

5 slices good peasant bread or grainy-type
    brown bread
4 tablespoons butter
4 tablespoons virgin olive oil
1½ tablespoons herbes de Provence
Salt and freshly ground pepper
1 small onion, sliced
1 clove garlic, minced finely
15 baby bella mushrooms, sliced thinly
Grated Parmesan cheese

1 Preheat the oven to 300°F. Slice off and discard the crusts of the bread . Cut each slice into four equal portions.

2 Place the butter in a bowl, add 2 tablespoons of the olive oil, the herbes de Provence, and salt and pepper to taste. Mix and cream well with a fork until the butter reaches a creamy consistency. Set aside

3 Pour the remaining 2 tablespoons of olive oil into a skillet and add the onion, garlic, and mushrooms. Sauté lightly for about 3 minutes.

4 Generously butter a cookie sheet or some ovenproof plates. Spread the herbed butter on the bread slices and place the canapés on the cookie sheet.

5 Evenly distribute the mushroom mixture on the buttered bread. Sprinkle with grated Parmesan. Bake the canapés for 6–8 minutes. Serve immediately.

Canapés with Roquefort and Walnuts

1 Preheat the oven to 300°F. Slice the baguette into two dozen equal slices. Generously butter a cookie sheet and place the slices on the cookie sheet.

2 Place the crumbled Roquefort cheese in a bowl and add the Cognac and mustard. With a fork, mix well until a creamy consistency is achieved. With a knife, spread this mixture evenly on the bread slices.

3 In a covered saucepan, boil the walnuts in water for about 5 minutes, until they are softened. Drain the walnuts on paper towels and then crumble them with a sharp knife.

4 Distribute the crumbled walnuts evenly over the cheese spread. Bake for about 6 minutes. Transfer the canapés to a serving plate and serve hot.

Makes 24 canapés

1 baguette or *ficelle* loaf
(long, thin French bread)
2 ounces Roquefort cheese, crumbled
1 1/2 tablespoons Cognac
1 1/2 tablespoons French mustard
1 1/2 cups walnuts

Stuffed
Avocados

2 ripe avocados

1 ripe tomato, seeded and chopped in very
   small chunks

1 celery stalk, from the heart or center of
   the celery, minced

20 pignoli (pine nuts)

1 shallot, minced

2 teaspoons tomato paste

3 tablespoons lemon juice

1 tablespoon olive oil

Salt and freshly ground pepper

4 large lettuce leaves

Finely chopped fresh cilantro, for garnish

1 Just before serving, cut each avocado length-wise into two equal halves. Remove the seed.

2 Place in a bowl the tomato, celery, nuts, shallot, tomato paste, lemon juice, olive oil, and salt and pepper to taste, and mix well. Check and adjust the seasonings. Keep the tomato mixture chilled until ready to serve.

3 Place a lettuce leaf on each of the four serving plates. Put an avocado half, hollow upward, on the top of each leaf. Fill the avocado hollow with the tomato mixture. Sprinkle cilantro on top of each avocado half. Serve immediately.

Minted Melon
with Yogurt

Makes 6 servings

3 small, ripe melons
4 tablespoons lemon juice
1 (16-ounce) container low-fat plain yogurt
Salt and freshly ground pepper
4 or 5 fresh mint leaves, finely minced

1 Slice each melon into two equal halves. Clean the insides and discard the seeds. Sprinkle a few drops of the lemon juice over each half.

2 Place the yogurt in a bowl, and add the remaining lemon juice, salt and pepper, and half of the mint.

3 Just before serving, fill each melon hollow with the yogurt mixture. Sprinkle each serving with additional chopped mint. Serve cold.

NOTE: It is particularly appetizing and refreshing during the hot-weather months.

Languedoc Dip

1 Place the shallots, spinach, watercress, chervil, parsley, and tarragon in a casserole. Add the water and boil for exactly 1 minute. Drain in a colander or sieve and then run cold water over the spinach mixture. Drain again.

2 Place the spinach mixture in a food processor. Add the chives, capers, cucumber, and garlic. Blend thoroughly.

3 Place in a deep bowl. Add the egg, sour cream, and olive oil. Blend all the ingredients well by hand with the help of a fork. Cover and place in the refrigerator until ready to serve.

NOTE: This delicious dip can be used in many creative ways: Spread over baguette slices or crackers. Use it to fill the center of hard-boiled eggs. Or use it as a dip with fresh vegetables such as broccoli, cauliflower, carrots, celery, and so on.

Makes one small bowl of dip

2 shallots, or 1 medium onion, chopped

10 spinach leaves, well washed

10 sprigs of watercress

5 sprigs chervil

5 sprigs parsley

A few tarragon leaves

3 cups water

5 chive stalks, chopped finely

12 capers

1 small cucumber pickle (cornichon)

2 small cloves garlic

1 hard-boiled egg, peeled and crumbled

1 (16-ounce) container low-fat sour cream

2 tablespoons virgin olive oil

Warm
Antipasto

Makes 4 servings

1 Preheat the oven to 350°F. Place the red and yellow peppers under the broiler and turn them often, until their skin becomes black and blistered. Remove them from the oven, place them in a paper bag for 10–15 minutes, then strip off the skin. Discard the skin, the stems, and the seeds. Set the peppers aside in an ovenproof dish.

2 Generously oil a 9 × 11-inch baking dish and place the zucchini, onions, tomatoes, and olives in the pan. Brush the top of the vegetables with olive oil and sprinkle with a little salt. Roast for about 20 minutes. During the last 5 minutes, place the dish of peppers in the oven to warm them.

3 Meanwhile, prepare a vinaigrette by mixing the oil, vinegar, and salt and pepper in a small bowl. Whisk until all the elements are well blended.

4 To serve, arrange decoratively on each of the four serving dishes: one red pepper half, one yellow pepper half, one zucchini half, one onion half, and two tomato halves. Place four black olives and two green olives on each dish, and sprinkle 1 teaspoon of capers over each dish. Pour the vinaigrette equally over the four portions, top each serving with finely chopped marjoram, and serve immediately—warm, or at least at room temperature.

2 large red bell peppers, cut in half lengthwise

2 large yellow bell peppers, sliced in half lengthwise

2 medium zucchini, sliced in half lengthwise

2 medium Vidalia onions, sliced in half lengthwise

4 medium ripe tomatoes, sliced in half lengthwise

16 pitted black olives

8 pitted green olives

¼ cup virgin olive oil, plus extra for brushing

4 tablespoons wine vinegar

Salt and freshly ground pepper

4 teaspoons capers

1 tablespoon fresh marjoram, chopped finely

Goat Cheese-
Fresh Herb Dip

Makes one small bowl of dip

12 ounces fresh goat cheese

8 tablespoons extra-virgin olive oil

1/2 cup low-fat sour cream or plain yogurt

2 teaspoons fresh thyme, minced

2 teaspoons fresh rosemary, chopped finely

3 tablespoons fresh parsley, chopped finely

3 tablespoons fresh chives, chopped finely

1 teaspoon fresh oregano, chopped finely

1 clove garlic, finely minced

1/2 teaspoon French mustard

Salt and freshly ground pepper

1 Place the cheese, oil, and sour cream in a blender or food processor. Blend well.

2 Place the cheese mixture in a deep serving bowl. Add all the herbs, the mustard, and salt and pepper to taste. Whisk and blend with a fork. Refrigerate the dip for several hours.

3 Serve the dip with baguette slices or crackers, or use it with fresh vegetables from the garden. It is delicious over tomato slices!

Asparagus–
Roasted Pepper
Canapés

Makes 24 canapés

$1/2$ pound fresh, thin asparagus

1 (8-ounce) jar roasted peppers

6 slices whole wheat bread

French mustard

6 slices Emmentaler or other Swiss cheese

Capers, for garnish

1 Preheat the oven to 300°F. Boil the asparagus in salted water for 2 minutes. Drain thoroughly. Slice the asparagus into 2-inch lengths and set aside.

2 Drain the peppers and slice them into thin pieces about 2 inches long.

3 Trim the crusts from the bread slices and spread a bit of mustard over each slice. Cut each slice into four equal parts.

4 Cut each cheese slice in four equal parts and place each on a portion of bread.

5 Generously butter an 11 × 7-inch ovenproof baking dish and place the cheese-topped bread in it. Arrange three asparagus strips on each canapé, two at the edges and one at the center. Between the asparagus strips place one thin red pepper piece. At the center of each canapé, place 2 capers on each side of the central strip of asparagus.

6 Bake the canapés for 8–10 minutes. Remove from the oven and serve warm.

Tapenade Provençale

Place all the ingredients except the oil in a food processor or blender. Add the olive oil gradually as the ingredients blend, until the mixture turns into a smooth paste. Taste and adjust the seasonings as needed; for example, add a bit of extra lemon juice or herbs de Provence, if necessary. Refrigerate until ready to serve.

NOTE: This wonderful creamy Provençale concoction can be served during the aperitif with thin slices of fresh country bread or French baguette, water crackers, and so on. I occasionally combine the tapenade with hard-boiled egg yolk to fill the inside of halved hard-boiled eggs.

Makes one small bowl of dip

1 pound pitted black olives, chopped

6 ounces capers

4 cloves garlic, peeled

2 tablespoons lemon juice

3 tablespoons herbes de Provence

Freshly ground pepper

A few sprigs parsley, chopped finely

3/4 cup extra-virgin olive oil

Eggplant Terrine

Makes 6 servings

1 Preheat the oven to 350°F. Pour the oil into a medium-size nonstick skillet, add the vegetables (including the garlic), and sauté over medium-low heat for about 10 minutes, stirring frequently. When the vegetables are done, crush them thoroughly with a masher, and set aside.

2 In a deep bowl, beat the eggs well and add the bread crumbs, herbs, and salt and pepper. Mix until well blended.

3 Add the vegetable mixture to the egg mixture and mix well.

4 Generously butter a 9 × 5-inch loaf pan and place the mixture in it. Bake for 25–30 minutes, then unmold carefully onto a serving plate. Allow to cool.

5 Slice the eggplant loaf carefully and pour some hot tomato sauce over each portion. Serve immediately.

NOTE: This dish is an excellent appetizer. It can be presented hot or cold. During the summer months, refrigerate and serve it cold. (The sauce, in that case, should also be served cold).

7 tablespoons virgin olive oil

1 pound eggplants, cut into chunks

4 red bell peppers, seeded and diced

3 medium onions, chopped coarsely

4 cloves garlic, minced

4 eggs

6 slices whole wheat bread, crumbled

3 tablespoons dried mixed herbs (basil, thyme, and rosemary)

Salt and freshly ground pepper

1 recipe Tomato Sauce (page 212), prepared and kept hot

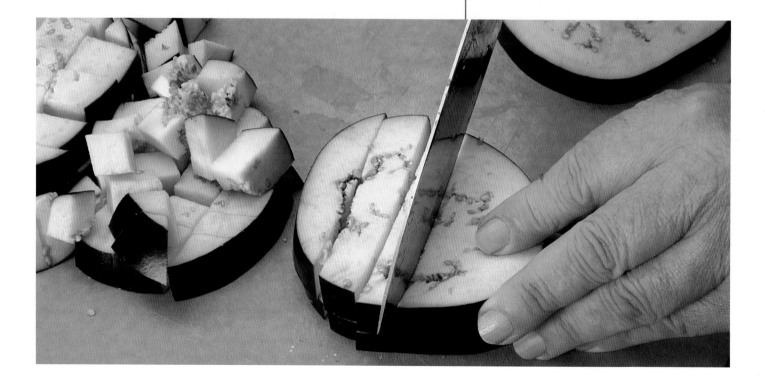

Spicy Black Bean Dip

Makes 10–12 servings

1 medium onion, chopped
1 (15-ounce) can black beans, drained
    and rinsed
3 cloves garlic, minced
1 green bell pepper, seeded and diced
1/3 cup chopped fresh cilantro
3 tablespoons lemon or lime juice
1 small jalapeño pepper, seeded and diced
1 tablespoon ground cumin
Salt
1 (8-ounce) container low-fat sour cream
Tortilla chips, for serving

1 Place all the ingredients, except the sour cream and chips, in a food processor. Blend well and transfer the mixture to a deep bowl.

2 Add the sour cream to the mixture and, with the help of a fork, blend well. Place the bowl, covered, in the refrigerator until the dip is ready to be served. Serve with tortilla chips.

Soups

Soup as a main course,
Soup to begin the meal,
And when it is homemade,
It is soup to nourish the soul.

—Julia Child, *The French Chef Cookbook*

From ancient times, soups have always held a conspicuous place in the daily fare of families and monasteries. This is still true today in many parts of the world, and it continues to be so in most of the Mediterranean countries—Italy, France, Spain, Greece, and so on—and the monasteries located there. The appeal of soups is universal. There is something so fundamental about soups, so much so that our basic instincts readily identify and feel drawn naturally to the magic of soups. It is almost as if soups are second nature to all of us.

Soups are always welcome at any time of the year: hot during the cold-weather months and cold during steamy hot periods. Throughout the years, I have always noticed how comforted guests feel at the monastery when a bowl of homemade soup is offered to them at their arrival. In many ways, that bowl of hot soup symbolizes the warmth and comfort they expect to find during their stay there.

The soup recipes presented here are an open invitation to the reader-cook to rediscover again and again the art of soup making. The recipes contained here are easy to experiment with, to subject to many adaptations and variations, and when carefully prepared they provide great enjoyment. I have always asserted, just as our ancestors did before us, that soup making is basic to everyday living, to life itself. Soup making is so intertwined with everything connected with the rhythm of work and our daily routines, the shift of the seasons, the size and distinct taste of families, time constraints, the particular quality and accent of an ordinary meal as that of a festive occasion. Besides all other considerations, soups are usually very healthy for all of us. They invariably contain lots of vitamins and fiber, sometimes absent in other culinary concoctions. And since soup bases are prepared with a variety of vegetables, they naturally provide us with a good intake of them, sometimes just the right amount needed as part of a healthy daily diet. When planning a menu, we find that no matter what, soups easily adapt themselves to any situation or circumstance, often bringing much comfort to those who consume them. As someone once said, soup remains a faithful friend during all of life's occasions.

I trust the discriminating cook or even the simple soup fan will enjoy trying these recipes and indulge in the pleasures of soup making. Enjoy not only the process of soup preparation, but go a bit further and extend this joy to your family and friends by sharing the results with them in a warm spirit of conviviality and friendship. As the French would say, invite them often *à la soupe*.

For the sake of losing a few pounds, accumulated during those endless agapes and festivities of the year's end, without having to fast or die of hunger, there is no better remedy than a good soup. All it takes is a quick stop at the supermarket, some preparation, and then promptly the fresh aromas begin to emerge from the soup kettle.

—Isabelle Delaleu, French chef and dietitian

Celery Bisque with Stilton Cheese

Makes 4 servings

3 tablespoons butter

4 cups sliced celery (about 8 stalks)

2 cups chopped leeks, well washed, white and pale green parts only (about 2 medium leeks)

$^3/_4$ pound Yukon Gold potatoes, peeled and diced

6 cups low-salt vegetable stock, plus more as needed

$^1/_3$ cup Crème Fraîche (page 216), plus 4–6 teaspoons for garnish

$^1/_2$ cup Stilton cheese, crumbled

$^1/_4$ teaspoon cayenne

Salt and freshly ground pepper

Chopped fresh parsley (optional)

1 Melt the butter in large, heavy pot over medium-high heat. Add the celery and leeks. Sauté until the celery is slightly softened, about 4 minutes. Add the potatoes and stock. Bring to a boil, then lower the heat to medium-low. Simmer, uncovered, until all the vegetables are tender, about 30 minutes.

2 Working in batches, puree the soup in a blender until smooth. Return to the pot and whisk in the $^1/_3$ cup of crème fraîche, and add the Stilton and cayenne. Reheat the soup, and season to taste with salt and pepper. Ladle the soup into four to six soup plates. Swirl 1 teaspoon of crème fraîche into each serving. Sprinkle with parsley, if desired. Serve hot.

Spicy Lentil Soup

Makes 6–8 servings

1 Place the lentils and rice in a bowl filled with water and set aside for 30 minutes. Rinse and drain.

2 Heat the oil in a large soup pot, then add the onions, celery, carrot, and tomatoes, and sauté lightly over medium heat, stirring continually. After 4 or 5 minutes, add the tomato paste and garlic. Cook, stirring, for another minute or two.

3 Add the lentil mixture, vegetable stock, salt and cayenne, paprika, lemon zest, and cumin. Stir well. Cover the pot and bring the soup to a boil. Allow it to boil for about 5 minutes.

4 Lower the heat to medium-low, stir, cover the pot, and allow the soup to simmer for 40–45 minutes, until the vegetables are thoroughly cooked. Check the seasonings, remove the lemon zest, and serve the soup hot. Place 1 tablespoon of yogurt at the center of each serving, surrounded by the cilantro.

2$^{1}/_{2}$ cups black lentils

$^{1}/_{2}$ cup uncooked long-grain rice

$^{1}/_{4}$ cup olive oil

4 onions, chopped finely

1 celery stalk, sliced thinly

1 large carrot, cut into small dice

2 tomatoes, peeled, seeded, and diced

3 tablespoons tomato paste

4 cloves garlic, minced

11 cups vegetable stock or water

Salt and cayenne

2 teaspoons paprika

1 long strip lemon zest

1 tablespoon ground cumin

6–8 tablespoons plain yogurt, for garnish

Finely chopped fresh cilantro, for garnish

Spring Soup

1 Heat the olive oil in a soup pot and sauté the onion. Cook over medium-low heat, stirring continually.

2 Dissolve the cornstarch in 1 cup of the vegetable stock and add it gradually to the onions. Add the remaining stock and the lemon juice and bring to a boil. Add the spinach, lower the heat to medium-low, cover, and simmer gently for 20 minutes. Allow the soup to cool for a few minutes, then add the remaining ingredients, except chervil, and stir well.

3 Blend the soup in a blender or food processor. Pour back into the pot and reheat it if you are planning to serve it hot. Otherwise, place it in the refrigerator for several hours and serve it chilled. Sprinkle with chervil before serving.

NOTE: This is an ideal soup to serve in spring, hence the name, or early summer. When the spinach is in season, it is best freshly harvested from the garden or purchased at a farmers' market.

Makes 4–6 servings

4 tablespoons olive oil

1 large onion, chopped finely

2 tablespoons cornstarch

6½ cups vegetable stock or water

2 tablespoons lemon juice

1 pound fresh spinach, well washed and chopped coarsely

1 (8-ounce) container low-fat sour cream

Salt and freshly ground pepper

A pinch grated nutmeg

Finely chopped fresh chervil, for garnish

Dutch Soup with Gouda Cheese

Makes 4–6 servings

3 tablespoons butter

4 apples, peeled, cored, and sliced thinly

2 leeks, well washed, white and pale green parts only, sliced thinly

1 tablespoon all-purpose flour

$1/2$ teaspoon grated nutmeg

$1/2$ teaspoon ground cinnamon

$1/2$ teaspoon ground cumin

2 cups water

2 cups milk

1 cup grated or shredded Gouda cheese

Salt and freshly ground pepper

Finely chopped fresh chervil, for garnish

1 Melt the butter in a large soup pan over medium-low heat. Add the apples and leeks. Sauté, stirring, for 4–5 minutes.

2 Add the flour and stir again. Add the nutmeg, cinnamon, and cumin, and stir well. Add the water, raise the heat to medium, stir well, and let the soup boil for 8–10 minutes.

3 Lower the heat to medium-low, add the milk and cheese, and continue to cook for another 5–6 minutes or so.

4 Pour the soup into a blender and whirl for a quick second or two. Return the soup to the pot and reheat, adding salt and pepper to taste. Stir well and serve hot, sprinkled with chervil.

Candlemas
Black-Eyed
Pea Soup

Makes 6–8 servings

8 tablespoons good vegetable oil or olive oil

2 leeks, well washed, white and pale green parts only, sliced thinly

1 large onion, chopped

4 carrots, peeled and diced

2 medium potatoes, peeled and diced

2 cups dried black-eyed peas

12 cups water

1 bay leaf

Salt and freshly ground pepper

A pinch ground cumin

$^1/_3$ cup fresh cilantro or parsley, minced finely, plus extra for garnish

1 Pour the oil into a soup kettle and sauté the leeks and onion for about 3 minutes.

2 Add the carrots, potatoes, black-eyed peas, water, bay leaf, salt and pepper, and cumin. Bring the soup to a boil, then lower the heat to medium-low. Cover the kettle and cook the soup for 1 hour, or until the peas are cooked. Stir from time to time, so nothing sticks to the bottom.

3 When the soup is done, allow it to cool for a while, and then blend in a blender or food processor until it achieves a smooth, creamy consistency. Return the soup to the pot and reheat, add the cilantro, and stir well. Check the seasonings, including the cumin. Do not let the soup come to a second boil. Serve the soup hot, sprinkled with additional cilantro.

NOTE: This soup takes its name from the feast of the Presentation of the Lord in the Temple, celebrated annually on February 2 by the churches of the east and west. This feast is commonly known in England as Candlemas, for candles play an important role in the day's liturgy. The theme of light permeates the entire celebration of the feast, evocative of the words of the elder Simeon who called the Christ Child, "a light to enlighten the nations." The candles are blessed at the beginning of the ritual and then carried by the faithful in the procession that follows, and later placed in front of the icon of the feast, where they represent the silent petitions of our prayers.

Creamy Sorrel Potage

1 Melt the butter in a soup pot and add the sorrel, lettuce, onion, and garlic. Cook over low heat, stirring constantly, until the vegetables gradually wilt and turn saucelike.

2 Add the water, salt and pepper, and thyme. Stir well and cover the pot. Bring the soup to a boil and then lower the heat to medium-low. Cook for about 20 minutes.

3 In a blender, mix the eggs with the milk. Pour into the soup and mix well. Continue to cook, stirring, but do not let the soup reach the boiling point. Serve hot, topped with croutons.

Makes 6 servings

4 tablespoons butter or margarine

6 cups thinly chopped and shredded fresh sorrel leaves

1 medium head Boston lettuce, shredded thinly

1 medium onion, chopped finely

2 cloves garlic, minced finely

4 cups water

Salt and freshly ground pepper

A pinch dried thyme

2 eggs

2 cups milk (for a richer version of the soup, use half-and-half)

Croutons, for garnish

INTRODUCTION TO THE MEAL

Potage Condé

Makes 6 servings

2 cups dried red beans, or 2 (15-ounce) cans
    kidney beans, drained and rinsed
2 large carrots, peeled and cubed
2 onions, chopped
2 cloves garlic, minced
9 cups water
1 bouquet garni (1 sprig each thyme and
    rosemary, and a bay leaf tied in a square
    of cheesecloth)
Salt and freshly ground pepper

1 Soak the dried beans overnight. Drain and place them in a soup kettle. Add the carrots, onions, garlic, water, and bouquet garni.

2 Bring the water to a boil, then cover the pot and lower the heat to medium-low. Cook for about 1 hour, stirring from time to time and adding more water if necessary.

3 After 1 hour, check to see if the beans are well cooked. Add the salt and pepper. Stir thoroughly, remove the bouquet garni, turn off the heat, and cover the pot until the soup cools.

4 Blend the soup in a blender or food processor in batches until it achieves an even, creamy consistency. Reheat the soup and serve hot.

Monastery
Watercress
Soup

Makes 4–6 servings

4 tablespoons butter

1 large Vidalia onion, chopped coarsely

6 green onions, trimmed and chopped

1 large potato, peeled and cubed

2 bunches watercress, trimmed, and
    chopped coarsely

⅓ cup all-purpose flour

4 cups vegetable stock

1 cup water

1 cup milk

Salt and freshly ground pepper

Finely chopped watercress (optional)

1 Heat the butter in a large soup kettle over medium-low heat. Gradually add the onion, green onions, potato, and watercress. Stirring frequently, cook for about 4 minutes, until the vegetables wilt and soften.

2 Add the flour and stir. Add the vegetable stock in small amounts, still stirring, and then add the water. Bring to a rapid boil and then, continuing to stir, cook for 12–15 minutes. Remove from the heat and allow to cool.

3 When the soup is cool or at room temperature, transfer to a blender and process in small batches until all the soup is blended.

4 Pour the soup back into the kettle and add the milk and salt and pepper to taste. Stirring well, reheat the soup. Serve hot and sprinkle watercress on top as a garnish, if desired.

Grandmother's
Garlic Soup

Makes 6 servings

1/2 cup virgin olive oil

16 cloves garlic, chopped coarsely

6 slices stale bread

6 cups vegetable stock or water

3 vegetable-flavored bouillon cubes (if water
    is used)

5 tablespoons tomato paste

1 tablespoon paprika

1 teaspoon ground cumin

Salt

A pinch cayenne

6 eggs

Finely chopped fresh parsley, for garnish

1 Pour the oil into a nonstick casserole or soup pot. Sauté the garlic over medium heat for about 1 minute. Do not let it brown. Transfer the garlic to a bowl and set aside. Leave the oil in the pot.

2 Fry the bread slices on both sides in the same garlic-flavored oil. Remove the bread and set the slices aside.

3 Pour the vegetable stock (or the water and bouillon cubes) into the casserole over the remaining oil. Add the tomato paste, paprika, cumin, salt, cayenne, and cooked garlic. Bring the soup to a boil. Cover, lower the heat to medium-low, and simmer for 20 minutes.

4 During the last 5 minutes that the soup simmers, break the eggs into the soup and poach them. Lay one bread slice in each soup plate, pour the soup over it, and place one egg on the top of each serving of bread. Sprinkle with parsley before serving. Serve hot.

Tourangelle
Soup

Makes 6 servings

1 Melt the butter in a soup pot. Add the leeks and sauté them lightly over medium-low heat for several minutes, stirring frequently.

2 Add the water, turnips, and potatoes, and bring to a boil. Cover the pot and let it simmer gently for about 50 minutes, stirring occasionally.

3 Add the peas, cabbage leaves, and salt and pepper to taste. Stir. Cover the pot and continue to simmer for another 50 minutes. Serve hot.

4 tablespoons butter

4 leeks, well washed, white parts only, sliced

8 cups water or vegetable stock

2 medium turnips, cubed

2 potatoes, cubed

1 cup fresh or frozen peas

6 white cabbage leaves, cut into small pieces

Salt and freshly ground pepper

Potato and Stilton Cheese
Soup

Makes 6 servings

4 large potatoes, peeled and cubed

3 leeks, well washed, white and pale green
    parts only, sliced thinly

Salt

3 cups water

3 cups milk

3 tablespoons good-quality olive oil

2 tablespoons all-purpose flour

$1/2$ cup chopped fresh parsley

Freshly ground white pepper

1 cup crumbled Stilton cheese

1 In a large soup pot, place the potatoes, leeks, and salt. Add the water and bring to a boil. Lower the heat to medium-low, cover the pan, and simmer until the potatoes and leeks are cooked. Turn of the heat and gently mash the mixture.

2 Add the milk and olive oil, then sprinkle with the flour while stirring constantly. Add the parsley and pepper. Cook over medium-low heat for about 20 minutes, stirring from time to time. When the soup thickens and turns bubbly, add the cheese and continue to stir until all ingredients are well blended. Remove from heat and serve immediately.

Hearty Chickpea
Soup

1 Place the chickpeas, onions, carrots, and bay leaf in a large soup kettle. Add 7 cups of the water. Over medium heat, bring the water to a boil. Simmer for 20 minutes.

2 Heat the oil in a separate saucepan. Add the garlic and tomatoes. Sauté for 4–5 minutes over medium heat, until the tomato mixture becomes saucelike.

3 Add the tomato mixture to the soup, along with the spinach, salt and pepper, and paprika. Add the remaining cup of water and again bring the soup to a boil. Cover and simmer over medium-low heat for 20 minutes. Serve the soup hot, sprinkled with parsley.

Makes 6 servings

1 (15-ounce) can chickpeas, drained and rinsed, or 1 cup precooked dried chickpeas, drained

2 onions, chopped finely

2 medium carrots, peeled and cubed

1 bay leaf

8 cups water

¹/₄ cup olive oil

4 cloves garlic, minced

3 tomatoes, peeled, seeded, and chopped coarsely

2 cups finely chopped, well-washed spinach

Salt and freshly ground pepper

¹/₂ teaspoon paprika

Finely chopped fresh parsley, for garnish

Potato-Onion
Alpine-Style Soup

Makes 4–6 servings

2 bunches green onions, trimmed
4 tablespoons vegetable oil
1 medium yellow onion, chopped coarsely
3 russet potatoes, peeled and quartered
6 cups vegetable stock
Salt and freshly ground pepper

1 Cut the green onions in half cross-wise, dividing them into white and green parts. Coarsely chop the white parts and set them aside. Finely chop the green parts and set those aside separately.

2 Heat the oil in a medium-size pot over medium heat. Add the yellow onion and chopped white parts of green onions and cook, stirring often with a wooden spoon, until soft, for 8–10 minutes. Add the potatoes and stock and season to taste with salt and pepper. Raise the heat to medium-high and bring just to a boil. Lower the heat to medium-low and simmer, stirring occasionally, until the potatoes are soft, for 30–35 minutes.

3 Allow the vegetables and stock to cool slightly; then, working in batches, puree them together in a blender. Return the puree to the pot and reheat over medium heat until hot. Garnish the soup with the chopped green parts of the green onions.

Monastery Harvest Soup

Makes 6–8 servings

6 tablespoons olive oil

3 leeks, well washed, white parts only,
    sliced thinly

2 large carrots, peeled and cubed

3 celery stalks, sliced thinly

6 cabbage leaves, shredded in julienne style

10 cups water

Salt

1 large potato, peeled and cubed

1 turnip, cubed

1 cup string beans, sliced into 1-inch pieces

1 cup fresh or frozen green peas

Freshly ground pepper

1 long loaf French bread (baguette)

Grated cheddar cheese

Finely chopped fresh parsley, for garnish

1 Pour the oil into a large nonstick soup pot. Add the leeks and sauté over medium-low heat for 2 or 3 minutes. Add the carrots, celery, and cabbage, and continue to cook for another minute or two, stirring all the while.

2 Add the water and salt. Bring the soup to a rapid boil, then lower the heat to medium, cover the pot, and continue to cook for about 15 minutes. Add the potato, turnip, string beans, peas, and pepper to taste. Preheat your oven to 350°F now. Lower the stovetop heat to medium-low, stir, cover the pot, and simmer for 30 minutes.

3 Just before the soup is done, slice the bread, place the slices on a baking sheet, and sprinkle the grated cheese on top of each slice. Bake for about 5 minutes.

4 When the soup is done, check the seasonings. Serve the soup hot, sprinkled with parsley. Place the bread on a serving plate and pass it around.

NOTE: This is a typical soup served at the monastery during the period of the harvest. Since we are blessed to have a good *potager*, that is, a kitchen garden, we make use of the variety of products from the garden at the time to make this soup. Sometimes we change a vegetable or two, depending on what the garden is producing at that time.

Easy
Couscous
Soup

Makes 6–8 servings

4 tablespoons olive oil

1 large onion, chopped finely

1 celery heart, chopped finely

4 savoy cabbage leaves, chopped finely or
  julienned

1 clove garlic, minced

1 cup uncooked couscous

8$\frac{1}{2}$ cups water or vegetable stock

1 vegetable-flavored bouillon cube (if water
  is used)

1 bay leaf

1 tablespoon tamari sauce

Salt and freshly ground pepper

Fresh thyme leaves, for garnish

1 Pour the oil into a soup kettle and add the onion, celery, cabbage, and garlic. Sauté lightly over medium-low heat for about 3 minutes, stirring often.

2 Add the couscous and mix well. Add the water, bay leaf, tamari sauce, and salt and pepper to taste, and bring the soup to a boil. Stir well, lower the heat to medium-low, cover, and allow the soup to simmer for 1 hour.

3 After 1 hour, remove the bay leaf, check the seasonings, and serve the soup hot, sprinkled with thyme.

Part Two

Main Courses

Egg Dishes, Crêpes and Pancakes, Casseroles, and Rice and Pasta

Egg Dishes

resh eggs are an integral part of our diet here in the monastery. We are blessed to have a sufficient number of chickens, ducks, and guinea hens at our monastic farm, and they assiduously provide the freshest of eggs consumed at the table. We not only eat these eggs ourselves but frequently give them as gifts to our friends and neighbors. In turn, we are often reminded by these people of the wonders and magic that the monastery eggs work in their kitchen. Our chickens are free range and eat only natural organic matter: grains and lots of greens, including some grass; thus they continue to lay eggs that are now famous for their superb taste and color. (The local greens seem to enrich the deep yellow-orange of the yolk)

Eggs are available all year-round, though at times, some of our chickens get a rest and stop laying from early winter to early February. Needless to say, we may not get an abundance of eggs during that time, but we always seem to find a few hidden in some obscure corner of the barn, so we are not totally deprived during those dark winter months. In the monastic diet, eggs and cheese often replace meat. As meat prices keep rising and its qual-ity is sometimes contested, I am surprised that more people don't learn to substitute eggs in their diet as a source of high-quality protein. Eggs are certainly more economical than meat, they are always plentiful in the local farmers' markets, and when they arrive truly fresh from the local farms, as they are here in our monastery, they are pure delight to the palate. Nutrition-wise, eggs provide a good amount of vitamins A, B (riboflavin), D, and E, as well as lots of minerals such as iron and phosphorous. When eaten smartly and in moderation, eggs go a long way to comple-ment a healthy and quality-oriented type of nutrition.

Some dietitians counsel against the inclusion of eggs in one's diet, arguing that they are high sources of cholesterol. Throughout the years, I have heard different and opposing opinions about this among medical people and dietitians. There seems to be a certain confusion about how many eggs should be included in one's diet or how often one should be allowed to eat them. I think it is safe to assume that most healthy people can probably follow the com-monsense approach of cooks throughout the centuries, and, with-out fear, learn to incorporate eggs with moderation into their own cooking. Most important from a health standpoint is that we must be sure the eggs we consume are as fresh and natural as possible.

An omelette is scrambled eggs or a softly golden memory; rich, moist and delectable. It is a meal to be set with pride before the most discriminating palate. . . . All you need is a pan or a sling, a couple of eggs, a little self-confidence and there it is —an omelette to call your own.

—Irena Chalmers, *Omelette Originals*

The French, who do not eat eggs for breakfast, have put much of their ingenuity into eggs for any meal. A French text-book on the subject is entitled *One Thousand Ways to Prepare Eggs.* . . . Indeed, they can be used in scores of ways: for main course lunch or supper dishes, or for an especially important breakfast or brunch.

—Julia Child, *The French Chef Cookbook*

[The egg] symbolizes fertility and beauty. It represents one of the most perfect of foods from just about every standpoint: nutrition, flavor and versatility. And it has an unrivaled ability to stand alone or to contribute to other dishes.

—Mark Bittman, "The Minimalist: Eggs Take Their Place at the Dinner Table" *New York Times*, October 4, 2006

Cheese Soufflé
Omelet

Makes 2–4 servings

6 eggs, separated

2 teaspoons water

$1/2$ tablespoon fresh lemon juice

Salt and freshly ground pepper

$2/3$ ounce butter

$1/2$ cup cheddar or Gruyère cheese,
  coarsely chopped

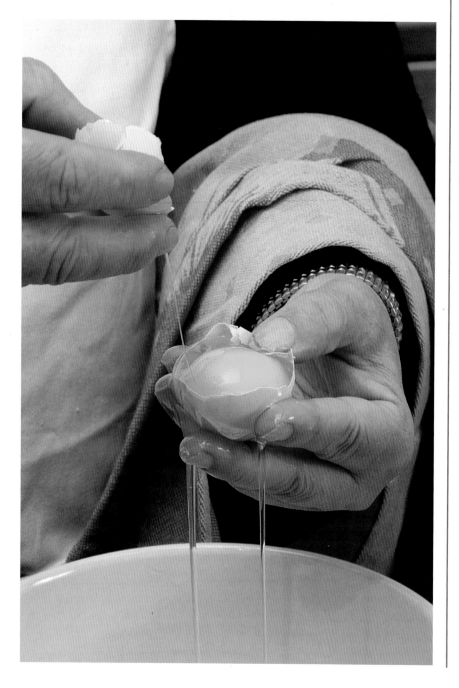

1 Place the egg yolks in a deep bowl and add the water, lemon juice, salt, and pepper. With an electric mixer, beat the egg mixture well until thoroughly blended. Wash and dry the beaters.

2 Place the egg whites in another deep bowl. Using clean beaters, beat the egg whites until stiff and firm. With a small spatula or spoon, gently fold the egg whites into the yolk mixture.

3 Preheat the grill to high.

4 Melt the butter in a deep ovenproof or cast-iron skillet. When the butter begins to foam, quickly add the egg mixture and swirl gently to spread it evenly. Cook for a minute or two. Remove from the heat and sprinkle the cheese all over the entire top.

5 Place the skillet under the grill for about 3 minutes, or until the cheese becomes puffed and golden. Carefully remove the skillet from the grill, cut into two to four equal pieces, and serve immediately.

Rousillon
Cheese Puff

Makes 4–6 servings

3 cups milk
Salt and freshly ground white pepper
$1/2$ cup whole wheat flour
$1/2$ cup coarse cornmeal
5 ounces New York or Vermont cheddar cheese
5 eggs, separated
$1/3$ cup Gruyère or mozzarella cheese, grated

1 Preheat the oven to 400°F. Pour the milk into a large saucepan. Add a pinch of salt and a pinch of pepper. Heat over medium-low heat. Gradually add the whole wheat flour while whisking steadily, then add the cornmeal, continuing to whisk steadily.

2 Continue to cook until the mixture achieves a thick, smooth consistency. At this point, add the cheddar cheese and mix well. Remove from the heat and allow to cool.

3 Beat the egg yolks and add them to the mixture. Add the Gruyère cheese and stir well, until all the ingredients are thoroughly blended.

4 Generously butter a 9 × 9-inch soufflé dish or another ovenproof dish. Pour the mixture into it. Beat the egg whites stiff and fold gradually into the mixture.

5 Lower the oven temperature to 350°F and bake for 25–30 minutes, until the top turns golden brown. Serve immediately.

Omelette
Saint-Girons

2 servings

2 ounces goat cheese
2 tablespoons fresh parsley, chopped finely
2 tablespoons fresh chives, chopped finely
2 tablespoons fresh chervil, chopped finely
5 eggs
Salt and freshly ground pepper

1 Combine the cheese and herbs in a bowl. Mash and mix them well with the help of a fork. Make sure the mixture is well blended.

2 In a separate bowl, beat the eggs lightly, add the salt and pepper, and beat some more.

3 Melt the butter in a nonstick omelet or crêpe pan over medium heat. Tilt the pan around until the butter covers the whole surface. Pour the egg mixture into the pan and tilt again until the mixture covers the entire surface. Cook for 4–5 minutes.

4 When the eggs are cooked, place the cheese mixture in the center of the omelet. Spread it with a spatula. Roll the omelet over the filling and enclose it gently. Slice the omelet in two perfect halves and serve immediately.

Scrambled Eggs Navarre Style

4–6 servings

14 tablespoons olive oil, divided

3 potatoes, peeled and diced

3 tomatoes, peeled, seeded, and chopped
    coarsely

2 onions, chopped

2 medium-size zucchini, diced

2 bell peppers, seeded and chopped finely

3 cloves garlic, minced

Salt

8 eggs

1/2 cup milk

Freshly ground pepper

1 Heat 6 tablespoons of the oil in a medium skillet, add the potatoes, and sauté the potatoes over medium-low heat, stirring occasionally. Sprinkle with salt. When the potatoes are done, turn off the heat, cover the pan, and keep them warm.

2 In a separate large skillet, heat the remaining 8 tablespoons of oil and combine the remaining vegetables. Sauté as you had the potatoes, stirring frequently and sprinkling with a pinch of salt.

3 In a large bowl, beat the eggs well, add the milk and salt and pepper, and beat again slowly with a mixer or by hand with a whisk or spoon.

4 Add the potatoes to the vegetable mixture and mix well. Pour the egg mixture over the vegetables and cook over medium heat, stirring often. When the eggs begin to set, remove the pan from the heat and serve immediately, while the eggs are still moist.

NOTE: Very often this dish is served in the Basque country on the top of a toasted slice of bread. No matter how you choose to serve it, this is an appetizing dish for a Sunday brunch or light lunch.

Asparagus Frittata Italian Style

4 servings

6 medium potatoes, peeled and sliced thinly
6 green onions
3 tablespoons olive oil
10 stalks fresh asparagus, trimmed and sliced
  into ½-inch lengths
2 tablespoons fresh parsley, chopped finely
Salt and freshly ground pepper
3 egg whites
5 whole eggs

1 Sauté the potatoes and green onions in the oil in a nonstick skillet over medium-low heat for several minutes. Stir and turn them over occasionally. (Don't overcook!)

2 Boil the asparagus in salted water for exactly 2 minutes. Drain thoroughly and add to the potato mixture. Mix well and continue to cook for an extra minute. Sprinkle with the parsley and salt and pepper, and mix again.

3 Whisk the egg whites in a bowl. Whisk the whole eggs in a larger bowl, add the egg whites, a pinch of salt, and pepper, and mix well. Pour the egg mixture over the vegetables in the skillet. When the eggs firm up, with the help of a spatula, turn the frittata over onto a large, flat plate. Slide the frittata back into skillet and cook the other side for about a minute. Slice the frittata in four equal slices and serve immediately.

Potato Omelet Nivernaise

Makes 4 servings

Olive oil

4 medium potatoes, peeled and sliced into
    very small dice

2 medium-size onions, chopped finely

2 bell peppers, seeded and chopped finely

8 eggs

Salt and freshly ground pepper

1 Heat four plates. Heat some oil in a large skillet and sauté the potatoes over medium-low heat.

2 When the potatoes are half-cooked (approximately 10 minutes), add the onions and bell peppers, and continue to cook, stirring continually. When the vegetables are cooked, remove them from the skillet. Set them aside and keep warm in a covered bowl.

3 Beat four of the eggs in a deep bowl, add salt and pepper, and beat some more. Pour some olive oil into the skillet (it is not necessary to wash in order to keep the flavor of the vegetables) and raise the heat to medium. When the oil is very hot, pour the egg mixture into the skillet, spreading evenly with a spatula. When the egg mixture sets firmly on the bottom, place half of the potato mixture in the center. Gently fold one half of the omelet over the other. Slice the omelet in half and serve immediately on the heated plates.

4 Repeat step 3 with the remaining eggs and potato mixture. (This recipe can also be used for making four individual omelets, by dividing the eggs and potato portions equally into four parts.)

Frittata for Saint Joseph's Day

Makes 4 servings

4 tablespoons butter

1 onion, chopped coarsely

1 carrot, peeled and finely grated

1 potato, peeled and sliced thinly

1 zucchini, sliced thinly

1 large tomato, seeded and chopped coarsely

7 eggs

$1/2$ cup heavy cream

Salt and freshly ground pepper

6 sprigs finely chopped fresh parsley

$1/4$ cup Parmesan cheese, grated

1 Preheat the oven to 300°F. Melt 2 tablespoons of the butter in a large cast-iron skillet. Add the onion, carrot, potato, zucchini, and tomato. Sauté over medium heat for a few minutes until the vegetables have softened, occasionally turning the potato and zucchini to cook them evenly.

2 Beat the eggs in a deep bowl, add the heavy cream, salt and pepper, parsley, and cheese, and beat some more until all the ingredients are well blended. Add the vegetables and mix well.

3 Clean and dry the skillet. Melt the remaining 2 tablespoons of butter in the skillet and tilt the pan to run it over the whole skillet bottom. When hot, pour the vegetable-egg mixture into the skillet and cook over medium-low heat until the bottom part seems well cooked (Check with a spatula). Transfer the pan to the oven. Bake until the top part is evenly cooked and solid. Remove from the oven, slice into four equal portions, and serve hot.

Matafam

Makes 4 servings

7 eggs

1½ cups milk

4 ounces flour, preferably whole wheat

Salt and freshly ground pepper

4 shallots, chopped finely

4 ounces butter

1 Preheat the oven to 350°F. In a deep bowl, beat the eggs. Add the milk and beat some more using an electric mixer, if possible. Add the flour and salt and pepper, and blend well. Add the shallots and mix by hand. Let the mixture rest at room temperature for 30 minutes.

2 Melt the butter in a large cast-iron skillet. Pour the egg mixture into it and cook over medium heat. When the bottom begins to set, transfer the pan to the oven and bake for 15–20 minutes, until the matafam is done. Serve hot.

NOTE: This peasant country dish, whose title means "kill the hunger"—*tue la faim* in French, crossed with the Spanish for that phrase, *mata el hambre*—comes from the Besançon region of France, an area that was for a long time occupied by Spanish troops during earlier centuries. Hence the origin of the name.

Trucchia

12 tablespoons olive oil, divided

$1/2$ pound Swiss chard, green parts only,
   chopped finely

1 onion, minced

6 eggs

$1/2$ cup Parmesan cheese, grated

Salt and freshly ground pepper

1 Pour 6 tablespoons of the olive oil into a large nonstick skillet, and heat over medium heat. When hot, add the chard and the onion. Cover and cook for about 2 minutes, then lower the heat to low, stir well, re-cover the skillet, and continue to cook for another 4 minutes or so, until the chard wilts and is thoroughly cooked.

2 In a deep bowl, beat the eggs, add the cheese and salt and pepper, and beat some more. Add the chard mixture and blend well.

3 Pour the remaining 6 tablespoons oil into a large nonstick skillet, and heat over medium heat. When hot, pour the egg mixture into it. Cover the skillet and cook for 2–3 minutes. When the bottom part is cooked, with the help of a spatula carefully transfer the *trucchia* to a large plate, then return it upside down to the skillet. Continue to cook until the lower part is done. Cut into four to six equal slices and serve. It can also be cut into small squares and served at room temperature with an aperitif.

Omelette de la Mère Poulard

Makes 2 servings

6 eggs, yolks and whites beaten separately
1 tablespoon water
Salt and freshly ground pepper
2 tablespoons heavy cream
3 tablespoons butter

1 Heat two plates. Place the egg yolks in a deep bowl. Add the water and salt and pepper, and beat thoroughly with a whisk or mixer.

2 In a separate bowl, place the egg whites, heavy cream, and a pinch of salt and pepper, and beat stiff with the help of a whisk or mixer.

3 Melt the butter in a medium-size skillet. When the skillet is well heated, pour the egg yolk mixture on the skillet and tilt the pan to help it run over the whole surface. When it begins to set, pour the egg white mixture over it and spread evenly with a spatula. Cover the skillet for 1 minute, moving constantly, then uncover and immediately fold one half the omelet carefully over the other half. Continue to cook for 30 seconds over medium-low heat. Cut the omelet in half and serve on the heated plates.

NOTE: This omelet, famous all over the world because of its association with the Mont St. Michel, was the creation of a certain Mme. Poulard, who passed on her secret recipe to her son. The secret is to move the skillet constantly while the omelet is being made; and of course, be sure to separate the egg yolks from the whites.

Eggs Cocotte in Pesto Sauce

Makes 6 servings

22 fresh basil leaves

5 teaspoons pignoli (pine nuts)

5 tablespoons olive oil

2 cloves garlic

5 cups heavy cream

6 eggs

Salt and freshly ground pepper

A pinch grated nutmeg

12 teaspoons grated Parmesan cheese

1 Preheat the oven to 300°F. Prepare the pesto sauce by mixing the basil, pignoli, olive oil, and garlic in a food processor. Process well and then pour the sauce into a bowl. Add the heavy cream and blend well by hand. Refrigerate the sauce until ready to serve.

2 Generously butter six ramekins. Cover the bottom of each ramekin with a bit of the pesto sauce. Break an egg in the center of each ramekin. Sprinkle salt and pepper and a pinch of nutmeg onto each egg. Cover the eggs with the rest of the pesto sauce. Sprinkle each ramekin with 2 teaspoons of Parmesan cheese.

3 Place the ramekins in a baking pan large enough to hold them. Carefully pour water into the pan around the ramekins, to about a 2-inch depth, or below the height of the ramekins. This creates a bain-marie. Bake the eggs in the bain-marie for about 10 minutes, maximum. When the eggs are ready, serve them immediately, accompanied by fresh French bread.

Crêpes and Pancakes

Crêpes are an integral part of *gastronomie normande*. Not surprisingly then, many of the recipes offered here have their origin in the cuisine of Normandy, a part of France I know well and where throughout the years I spent many long intervals in the company of cherished friends, some of whom still remain there. Many of these recipes don't exist in cookbooks; they are rather small treasures handed down from one generation to the other—a living tradition kept alive in the homes, inns, and restaurants of Normandy, especially at latter establishments actually called *crêperies*. Whenever crêpes are served at home in France, they imply a certain intimacy at the table among all family members the *cuisinier* wishes to pamper. The same principle applies to a gathering of friends in one's home, where conviviality is an integral part of the menu, or to a local restaurant where the chef wishes to treat his customers to something special.

Crêpes, in general, are not complicated to make, but their preparation demands a certain amount of time and the acquisition of certain techniques. Some of the recipes described here may require special ingredients, although the majority of them may be prepared with staples found at any local market. The crêpe batter is usually made in advance, from 2 to 4 hours before cooking, and then placed in the refrigerator to chill and thicken. Sometimes, a few drops of cold water are added just before cooking, to give the crêpes a lighter consistency.

When one is involved in crêpe preparation, it is always advisable to use a traditional cast-iron crêpe pan with sloping sides. Sometimes they differ in size and diameter, and here in the monastery we have at least three different sizes of crêpe pans. To keep cooked crêpes warm before serving, place them in a warm oven (about 250°F) until they are ready to be served. Crêpes can be something well planned, days ahead of time, or the unique invention of the moment. If made in advance, they can be stored in the refrigerator for several days before using them. In that case, since they tend to be of a delicate nature, wrap them well in foil and shelve them with care. If they are to be served hot, for example, as part of the main course, they should be placed either in the oven or under the broiler for a few minutes before they are served.

Crêpes are both light and delicious as a meal, and thus they often make a perfect, versatile dish to serve as a main course. They can be filled with diverse vegetable combinations; with ham, chicken, or seafood; or with cheese, especially the famous Camembert, as they usually are in Normandy. They can also be used as dessert with apple or other fruit fillings, or on special occasions, with a thick chocolate sauce or something similar, at times topped with some ice cream. The selection for the fillings always depends on the talent and creativity of a good *cuisinier*.

> The crêpe, that famous thin light French pancake, is any cook's good friend. Crêpes cook in a minute or less, and can be made hours before serving. Not only hours, but weeks and months ahead since crêpes freeze perfectly . . . Anything goes in crêpes, including a soufflé, and this dramatic dish also makes a dashing dessert.
>
> —Julia Child, *The Way to Cook*

Cabbage-Potato
Pancakes

1 Preheat the oven to 250°F. Quarter the cabbage and steam for 6–7 minutes. Drain and chop finely.

2 Place the cabbage, potatoes, and onion in a large bowl. Mash thoroughly with a masher and mix well with a spatula.

3 Beat the eggs in separate deep bowl. Add the milk and beat some more. Add the vegetable mixture, salt and pepper, and parsley. Mix well until thoroughly blended.

4 To prepare the pancakes, use a crêpe pan or nonstick skillet. Heat about 1 tablespoon of oil (you will need to re-oil each time) and pour about one-eighth of the potato mixture into the pan. Flatten the mixture evenly with the help of a spatula and cook over medium heat until the pancake browns on the bottom. Turn over the pancake carefully and cook the other side. When the pancake is done, slide it carefully onto an ovenproof platter. Repeat the process until all the pancakes are done, keeping the cooked pancakes warm in the oven until ready to serve them. Before serving, sprinkle with parsley.

Makes about 8 pancakes

½ small green cabbage

4 large potatoes, peeled and grated

1 medium onion, finely minced

4 eggs

¾ cup milk

Salt and freshly ground pepper

1 small bunch fresh parsley, chopped finely

About 8 teaspoons vegetable or olive oil

1 Preheat the oven to 250°F. Place the potatoes into a pot and cover with cold water. Drain the potatoes just before using them.

2 Beat the eggs in a deep bowl, add the milk, and beat some more. Add the potatoes, onion, salt and pepper, thyme, and parsley. Mix well with the help of a spatula until thoroughly blended.

3 To prepare the pancakes, use a crêpe pan or nonstick skillet. Heat about 1 tablespoon of oil (you will need to re-oil each time) and pour about one-eighth of the potato mixture into the pan. Flatten the mixture evenly with the help of a spatula and cook over medium heat until the pancake browns on the bottom. Turn over the pancake carefully and cook the other side. When the pancake is done, slide it carefully onto an ovenproof platter. Repeat the process until all the pancakes are done, keeping the cooked pancakes warm in the oven until ready to serve them. Before serving, sprinkle with dill.

Le Puy Potato
Pancakes

Makes about 8 pancakes

5 large red potatoes, peeled and grated

3 eggs

$2/3$ cup milk

1 onion, grated or chopped finely

Salt and freshly ground pepper

$1/2$ teaspoon dried thyme

1 small bunch fresh parsley, chopped finely

About 8 teaspoons vegetable or olive oil

Finely minced fresh dill, for garnish

Sweet Potato Pancakes with Eggs

Makes 4 servings

4 large sweet potatoes

2 green onions, chopped finely

A bunch of fresh parsley, chopped finely

7 eggs

⅓ cup milk

Salt and freshly ground pepper

2 tablespoons butter

4 tablespoons oil

1 Boil the potatoes for about 15 minutes, or bake them at 350°F for 25–30 minutes. When they are done, run cold water over them, and allow them to cool for several hours.

2 Peel and mash the potatoes, or grate them in a food processor. Place them in a deep bowl, then add the green onions and parsley. Mix well.

3 Preheat the oven to 250°F. In a separate bowl, beat 3 of the eggs, add the milk and salt and pepper, and beat well. Pour this mixture into the bowl of potatoes and mix well. Refrigerate for at least 2 hours before continuing.

4 Heat the butter and oil in a large nonstick skillet. When the skillet is very hot, lower the heat to medium-low. Pour one-quarter of the potato mixture into the skillet, and with the help of a spatula press the mixture down evenly. Try to keep the pancakes circular. Cook for 4–5 minutes each side. (Flip carefully by sliding onto a plate, then turning the pancake over onto the skillet to cook the other side). Repeat the process three more times. Keep the pancakes warm in the oven until ready to eat.

5 Fry the remaining 4 eggs sunny-side up. Sprinkle with a pinch of salt and pepper. Distribute the pancakes among four individual plates, place an egg on the top of each, and serve.

NOTE: This is an ideal dish for a Sunday brunch or a light supper.

Crêpes Camembert à la Bretonne

1 Prepare the batter: In a deep large bowl, mix the eggs, oil, flour, and salt, and beat with a mixer, adding the milk gradually. The batter must reach the consistency of heavy cream and should be free of flour lumps. Add the water and continue to mix until the batter is light and smooth. Refrigerate the batter for an hour or two before continuing.

2 Preheat the oven to 300°F. Heat a 6- or 8-inch crêpe skillet over high heat and lightly grease the entire skillet with a bit of melted butter (or oil if preferred), by using a small pastry brush or by tilting the pan until the surface is completely greased. Using a small ladle, pour the batter into the skillet. Tilt it immediately so that the batter covers the entire bottom of the skillet and quickly becomes firm. Cook the crêpe for about 1 minute, until it begins to show signs of turning brown around the rim. Turn it over rapidly with a spatula and cook the reverse side for another minute. When the crêpe is done, slide it gently onto a flat plate. Brush the skillet once more with melted butter and repeat the process until all crêpes are made. You should have about 12 crêpes.

3 Prepare the filling: Melt the butter in a large nonstick skillet and add the mushrooms and onions. Sauté gently over medium-low heat for about 3 minutes, stirring frequently. Add the spinach and salt and pepper, and continue to cook for about 2 minutes, until the spinach wilts. Add the Camembert and heavy cream. Toss and mix the ingredients. Remove the skillet from the heat.

4 Generously butter a large baking dish. Fill the crêpes with the mushroom mixture, roll them up, and place them carefully in the dish, one next to the other. When all the crêpes are arranged in the dish, top them with heavy cream and bake for 15–20 minutes. Serve hot, allowing two crêpes per person.

Makes 6 servings

Batter:

4 eggs

2 tablespoons vegetable oil

1¼ cups flour, half whole wheat and half all-purpose

A pinch salt

3 cups milk

½ cup water

Filling:

3 tablespoons butter

½ pound mushrooms, sliced thinly

1 medium onion, sliced thinly

30 spinach leaves, well washed and chopped

Salt and freshly ground pepper

1 ounce Camembert cheese, cut into thin slices

2 tablespoons heavy cream, plus 2 additional tablespoons for topping

Crêpes
with Mushroom Filling

1 Prepare the batter: In a deep large bowl, mix the eggs, oil, flour, and salt, and beat with a mixer, adding the milk gradually. The batter must reach the consistency of heavy cream and should be free of flour lumps. If the batter is too thick, add 1 or 2 teaspoons of cold water and continue to mix until the batter is light and smooth. Refrigerate the batter for an hour or two before continuing.

2 Prepare the filling: Heat the butter in a large nonstick skillet over medium-low heat. Add the mushrooms and onion. Sauté for 4–5 minutes, until they begin to turn color. Stir well. In a small bowl, add the parsley to the Béchamel Sauce and mix well. Add the sauce to the mushrooms and stir the sauce thoroughly.

3 Preheat the oven to 300°F. Heat a 6- or 8-inch crêpe skillet over high heat and lightly grease the entire skillet with a bit of melted butter (or oil if preferred), by using a small pastry brush or by tilting the pan until the surface is completely greased. Using a small ladle, pour the batter into the skillet. Tilt it immediately so that the batter covers the entire bottom of the skillet and quickly becomes firm. Cook the crêpe for about 1 minute, until it begins to show signs of turning brown around the rim. Turn it over rapidly with a spatula and cook the reverse side for another minute. When the crêpe is done, slide it gently onto a flat plate. Brush the skillet once more with melted butter and repeat the process until all crêpes are made. You should have about 12 crêpes.

4 Generously butter a large baking dish. Fill the crêpes with the mushroom mixture, roll them up, and place them carefully in the baking dish, one next to the other. When all the crêpes are in the dish, spread the cream or half-and-half over the top, and bake for 20–25 minutes. Serve hot, allowing 2 crêpes per person.

Makes 4–6 servings

Batter:

4 eggs

2 tablespoons olive oil

1 1/4 cups all-purpose flour

A pinch salt

3 cups milk

1/2 cup heavy cream or half-and-half

Filling:

4 tablespoons butter

1 pound mushrooms, trimmed and sliced

1 onion, chopped coarsely

1/3 cup fresh parsley, finely chopped

1 cup prepared Béchamel Sauce (page 206)

Crêpes à la Ratatouille

1 Prepare the batter: In a deep large bowl, mix the eggs, oil, flour, and salt, and beat with a mixer, adding the milk gradually. The batter must reach the consistency of heavy cream and should be free of flour lumps. If the batter is too thick, add 1 or 2 teaspoons of cold water and continue to mix until it is light and smooth. Refrigerate the batter for an hour or two before continuing.

2 Prepare the filling: Heat the oil in a medium-size cast-iron or nonstick pot over medium heat. Add the onions and sauté for about 4 minutes, until they begin to turn color. Add the eggplant and zucchini and continue to sauté for about 4 minutes. Add the tomatoes, red pepper, garlic, thyme, rosemary, bay leaf, sage, paprika, and salt and pepper, and stir well. Lower the heat to medium-low, cover, and continue to cook, stirring from time to time, until the vegetables are tender and all the flavors have well blended. The cooking time should be between 30 and 40 minutes. When the ratatouille is done, discard the thyme and rosemary sprigs, and the bay leaf. Allow the ratatouille to cool a bit before filling the crêpes.

3 Preheat the oven to 300°F. Heat a 6- or 8-inch crêpe skillet over high heat and lightly grease the entire skillet with a bit of melted butter (or oil if preferred), by using a small pastry brush or by tilting the pan until the surface is completely greased. Using a small ladle, pour the batter into the skillet. Tilt it immediately so that the batter covers the entire bottom of the skillet and quickly becomes firm. Cook the crêpe for about 1 minute, until it begins to show signs of turning brown around the rim. Turn it over rapidly with a spatula and cook the reverse side for another minute. When the crêpe is done, slide it gently onto a flat plate. Brush the skillet once more with melted butter and repeat the process until all crêpes are made. You should have about twelve crêpes.

4 Generously butter a large baking dish. Fill the crêpes with ratatouille, roll them up, and place them carefully in the baking dish, one next to the other. When all the crêpes are in the baking dish, spread the cream or half and half over the top, and cover the dish with foil and bake for about 20 minutes. Serve hot, allowing two crêpes per person.

Makes 6 servings

Batter:

4 eggs

2 tablespoons olive oil

1¼ cups all-purpose flour

A pinch of salt

3 cups milk

½ cup heavy cream or half and half

Filling:

4 tablespoons extra-virgin olive oil

2 large onions, chopped coarsely

2 medium eggplants, cubed

3 medium zucchini, cubed

2 pounds ripe tomatoes, seeded and
  chopped coarsely

1 sweet red pepper, seeded and cut into
  small pieces

3 cloves garlic, minced

3 sprigs chopped or 2 tablespoons dried thyme

2 sprigs chopped or 1 tablespoon dried
  rosemary

1 bay leaf

A few sage leaves, crushed

½ teaspoon paprika

Salt and freshly ground pepper

Casseroles

asserole dishes are among the one-pot meals whose origins go back to antiquity, when ordinary cooking took place in an open hearth or primitive brick or stone oven. When industrial advances arrived in the nineteenth century, slowly but surely, kitchen ranges with built-in ovens started to take the place of previous cooking practices. The preparation of a casserole dish thus moved from the outdoors to the hearth and finally into the modern gas or electric oven.

Casseroles are very traditional dishes; they are also practical ones. For instance, a large casserole dish, filled with all sorts of ingredients, can go a long way to feed a large family or community. This is one reason why casserole dishes are often served in monasteries, especially in the winter. Casseroles also come handy when there are lots of leftovers . . . simply combine them with other vegetables, a staple such as cooked rice or noodles, and some eggs or cheese for protein, and you end up with a complete meal, or as the French love to call it, *un repas complet.*

Casserole dishes often include robust ingredients, such as beans or lentils, whose taste usually improves throughout the longer, slow process of oven-cooking. It is important to pay attention to whether all the food elements used in a casserole dish blend well and actually improve through the magic of baking. Take a good lasagna, for example; it needs the right type of filling that would go well with the other ingredients: the cheeses, the pasta noodles, and the sauce. One can't choose just any vegetable or meat preparation for the filling—it always needs to be the *right one*, to obtain a good result. Another important element for a good casserole, and one sometimes neglected, is sufficient and good-quality cheese—which produces the au gratin, the crust, or a good *croute*, as the French say. There is nothing lovelier or more appealing in a good casserole dish than to have this unique texture on top. I never hesitate to sprinkle casseroles with enough grated cheese to create a good *croute*. It is always appreciated at the table. Bread crumbs are also a good resource for creating a good *croute*, and sometimes the combination of both cheese and bread crumbs creates the type of *croute* one never forgets. It is small details such as these that are essential for a good casserole dish. One must also follow the directions in each recipe, such as the right oven temperature, the exact baking time, and the right type of ovenproof dishes for baking, to achieve success. Otherwise, the intended dish can end up a disaster!

The recipes presented here are quite easy to make and don't require a long preparation. They are often a great help when one needs to prepare a meal on the spur of the moment. Often, when the casserole contains all the elements of a complete meal, a soup or fresh salad or both, plus a simple dessert such as a piece of fruit, are all one needs to be totally satisfied.

A staple of French home cooking, gratins have long played a role similar to our casseroles.

Since they can be assembled ahead and are baked and served in the same dish, gratins make menu planning easy . . . It is the crust that forms during baking that gives the gratin its name. The French *gratiner* means to bake until crusty. Gratin has been extended to mean any dish, most often of vegetables and usually sprinkled with a topping, that obtains a crusty surface after being baked or broiled. Depending on the topping used, the crust can be delicate or crunchy. The traditional topping is grated Parmesan or Gruyère cheese or bread crumbs.

—Faye Levy, *Fresh from France*

Broccoli-Cheese
Casserole à la Duchesse

Makes 6 servings

1 Preheat the oven to 350°F. Boil the broccoli for about 10 minutes. Drain and then chop coarsely, including the stems.

2 In a small bowl, stir the milk and the cornstarch well, until the starch dissolves. Beat the eggs in a deep bowl. To the eggs, add the cheeses and the cornstarch mixture, and beat well. Add the onion, salt and pepper, and the broccoli, and mix well.

3 Generously butter an 8 × 8-inch ovenproof baking dish and place the broccoli mixture in it. Bake for about 30 minutes. Serve hot.

4 medium broccoli heads

1/2 cup milk

1 tablespoon cornstarch

3 eggs, beaten

1 cup ricotta cheese

1/3 cup cheddar cheese, grated

1 medium onion, chopped

Salt and freshly ground pepper

Polente Savoyarde

Makes 6 servings

6 cups milk

3 cloves garlic, crushed with a knife but
    left whole

3 tablespoons butter

Salt

A pinch grated nutmeg

1½ cups coarse cornmeal

3 eggs

2 ounces Parmesan cheese, grated, plus
    additional for topping

2 ounces Gruyère cheese, grated

Freshly ground pepper

1 In a large saucepan, preferably a nonstick one, bring the milk to a boil, then lower the heat to medium-low. Add the garlic, butter, a pinch of salt, and the nutmeg, and stir well.

2 When the butter has melted, add the cornmeal gradually while stirring continually to prevent the creation of lumps. Continue to stir with either a whisk or spatula until all the cornmeal is added and the polenta begins to thicken. Lower the heat to low. Continue to cook for 5–6 minutes, continuing to stir. At this point, check the consistency of the polenta to see if it needs a bit more milk or cornmeal. (Sometimes polenta can be a bit temperamental.)

3 In a deep bowl, beat the eggs thoroughly with a mixer, and add them gradually to the polenta while stirring continually. Stir for several minutes.

4 Remove the polenta from the heat, and remove and discard the garlic cloves. Add the cheeses and ground pepper and mix thoroughly with the help of a spatula. Allow the polenta to cool for at least 1 hour.

5 Preheat the oven to 300°F. Generously butter an 11 × 7-inch ovenproof dish and spread the polenta evenly in the dish. Run the spatula over the top several times to level it off. Sprinkle the extra Parmesan cheese over the whole top. Bake for 15–20 minutes. Serve hot. During the summer months, the prepared polenta can be refrigerated and served cold.

NOTE: Polenta, being a traditional dish of northern Italy, was naturally adopted in Savoy during the centuries that it was governed by the dukes of Savoy, who were attached to what eventually became Italy.

Saint Mary's Lentil and Roasted Vegetable Loaf

1 Preheat the oven to 400°F. Assemble the zucchini, peppers, and onions in a baking dish. Sprinkle with the olive oil and rosemary. Toss gently. Spread the vegetables evenly in the dish and cover with foil. Bake for 20–25 minutes, until the vegetables are tender. Remove from the oven and let cool.

2 Lower the heat to 350°F. In a large, deep bowl, combine the cooked lentils, mozzarella, bread crumbs, oregano, thyme, basil, salt, pepper, and 1 cup of the roasted vegetables. Mix well.

3 In a separate bowl, combine $1/2$ cup of the ketchup, the eggs, and the wine, and whisk by hand or with a mixer until well blended. Add the lentil mixture, and with the help of a wooden spoon stir until all is well blended. Generously butter or oil a 9 × 5 × 3-inch loaf pan and pour the mixture into it, leveling the mixture with the wooden spoon.

4 Pour the remaining $1/2$ cup of ketchup evenly over the top of the loaf. Bake for 50–60 minutes. Remove from the oven and let the pan stand for 15 minutes. Warm in a skillet the remaining unbaked vegetable mixture. Cut the loaf into equal slices. Place some of the vegetable mixture on top of each slice and serve immediately.

Makes 6–8 servings

3 medium zucchini, diced

3 red or green bell peppers, seeded and diced

2 medium red onions, chopped finely

4 teaspoons olive oil

2 tablespoons finely chopped fresh rosemary

2 cups cooked lentils

2 cups coarsely grated mozzarella cheese

$1^1/2$ cups bread crumbs

$1/2$ teaspoon dried oregano

$1/2$ teaspoon dried thyme

$1/2$ cup thinly sliced and chopped fresh basil

Sea salt

$1/2$ teaspoon freshly ground pepper

1 cup ketchup

3 eggs

$1/4$ cup dry white wine

Country-Style Broccoli-Potato Casserole

Makes 6–8 servings

1 Preheat the oven to 350°F. Boil the broccoli for 8–10 minutes. Drain and then chop coarsely, including the stems. Set aside.

2 Boil the potatoes for about 5 minutes. Drain and set aside.

3 In a deep bowl, dissolve the cornstarch in the milk, stirring. Add the beaten eggs, cheese, salt and pepper, and nutmeg. Mix well.

4 Add the broccoli and the potatoes to the egg mixture and, with a spatula, mix gently but well.

5 Generously butter an 11 × 7-inch ovenproof dish. Pour the mixture into it and distribute the ingredients evenly. Cover the top lightly with bread crumbs. Bake for 30 minutes. Cut into six to eight equal portions and serve hot.

4 medium broccoli heads

4 medium potatoes, peeled and cubed

1 cup milk

3 tablespoons cornstarch or all-purpose flour

3 eggs, beaten

1/2 cup grated mozzarella cheese

Salt and freshly ground pepper

A pinch grated nutmeg

Bread crumbs

Egg Noodle–
Asparagus Casserole

Makes 4–6 servings

12 ounces uncooked egg noodles

3 tablespoons butter

2 tablespoons cornstarch

2 cups whole or low-fat milk

Salt and freshly ground pepper

A pinch grated nutmeg

$1/2$ cup cheddar cheese, chopped and crumbled

2 cups cooked asparagus, cut into 2-inch pieces

1 (14-ounce) jar cocktail onions, drained

$1/2$ cup bread crumbs

1 Preheat the oven to 350°F. Cook the egg noodles in boiling salted water, according to directions on the package. Drain.

2 While boiling the noodles, melt the butter in a saucepan; dissolve the cornstarch in the milk in a small bowl; then gradually add it to the butter, stirring, until the sauce thickens. Add the nutmeg and cheese, and stir some more until all the cheese is melted.

3 Mix the asparagus and onions together in a bowl.

4 Generously butter a shallow baking dish and alternate layers of noodles, the asparagus mixture, and the sauce. You should have least two layers of each.

5 After spreading the sauce evenly over the last asparagus layer, cover the entire top surface with bread crumbs. Season with salt and pepper. Bake for 25–30 minutes, maximum. Serve hot.

Green
Polenta

makes 6 servings

6 cups water

Salt

2 small heads broccoli, chopped coarsely into
      small pieces

4 tablespoons olive oil

1 onion, chopped finely

2 cloves garlic, minced

1 $\frac{1}{2}$ cups coarse cornmeal

Freshly ground pepper

3 tablespoons butter

$\frac{1}{3}$ cup grated Parmesan cheese

1 Pour 3 cups of salted water in a large saucepan and add the broccoli. Bring to a boil. Lower the heat to medium-low. Cover and simmer gently for 15 minutes. Drain the broccoli, reserving the water.

2 Oil a skillet, add the onion and garlic, and sauté gently for about 2 minutes over medium-low heat. Turn off the heat and set aside.

3 Pour 3 cups of salted water in a large nonstick saucepan and bring to a boil. Add the reserved broccoli water to the boiling water in the saucepan. Sprinkle in the cornmeal gradually, stirring constantly. Continue until all the cornmeal is added. Keep stirring until a thick, even consistency is achieved. Turn off the heat.

4 Add the broccoli, the onion mixture, pepper to taste, the butter, and the Parmesan cheese. Mix well. Refrigerate for at least an hour.

5 Preheat the oven to 350°F. Generously butter an 11 × 7-inch ovenproof dish. With a spatula, spread the polenta evenly in the dish. Sprinkle more grated cheese on top. Bake for 20–25 minutes. Allow to cool a bit before serving.

NOTE: During the summer months, this polenta dish can be prepared in advance, refrigerated, and served cold.

Jubilate Loaf

1 Preheat the oven to 375°F. Boil the lentils in salted water in a large saucepan until they are cooked, about 20 minutes. Drain thoroughly and set aside.

2 While the lentils are boiling, pour the olive oil into a large nonstick skillet and add the onion, celery, and red pepper. Sauté over medium-low heat for 4–5 minutes, until the vegetables wilt. Turn off the heat. Add the garlic, rosemary, parsley, and tomato sauce. Mix well.

3 In a deep bowl, mix the bread crumbs and grated cheese together. Set aside.

4 In a large mixing bowl, beat the eggs, add the salt and pepper, and mix well. Add the lentils and mix again. Add the onion mixture and mix some more. Add the bread crumb mixture and mix thoroughly until well blended. Shape the mixture into a loaf.

5 Generously butter a 9 × 5 × 3-inch loaf pan and slide the loaf into it. (Reshape the loaf to fit the pan, if need be.) Place an elongated baking pan in the oven, add several cups of water (do not fill it), and place the lentil loaf in the center, to create a bain-marie. Bake for 45–50 minutes. The loaf is done when the top is browned and forms a crust. To be doubly sure, insert a thin knife into the loaf; if the knife comes out clean, the loaf is done.

6 Remove the loaf from the oven, allow it to cool for a few minutes, then unmold by carefully turning it upside down onto a platter. Slice and serve.

Makes 6–8 servings

2 cups dried French green lentils (if possible, Le Puy)

4 tablespoons olive oil

1 large onion, chopped coarsely

1 cup celery, chopped finely

1 large sweet red pepper, seeded and chopped finely

2 cloves garlic, minced

2 teaspoons dried rosemary

1/2 cup finely chopped fresh parsley

1/2 cup plain tomato sauce

1 cup dry bread crumbs

1/2 cup grated cheddar cheese

3 eggs

Salt and freshly ground pepper

Eggplant
Casserole Tirolese Style

1 Preheat the oven to 350°F. Spread a paper towel over a surface, and place the eggplants on the paper. Sprinkle some salt over them and leave them alone for 30 minutes.

2 In the meantime, place the potatoes in a large saucepan and add slightly salted water to cover. Bring to a boil, cover, and simmer for 10 minutes. Drain. It is important that the slices remain firm, so do not overcook them.

3 Pour the oil into a large nonstick skillet, add the onions, and sauté over medium-low heat for 2–3 minutes. Add the garlic, bell pepper, and parsley, and continue to sauté, stirring, for another 4–5 minutes, until the vegetables soften. Sprinkle with salt and pepper and the paprika, and mix well.

4 Generously butter a 13 × 9-inch ovenproof casserole. Make three sets of vegetable layers, each set starting at the bottom with the potatoes, followed by the eggplants, followed by the onion mixture, followed by the tomato slices. Sprinkle a few drops of oil and vinegar over the top. Repeat the layers twice more, following the same process.

5 Cover the top of the casserole with foil and bake for 50–60 minutes. Remove the foil during the last 10 minutes and allow the very top to brown. Serve the dish hot during the cold-weather months, or chill and serve cold during the summer.

Makes 6–8 servings

2 medium eggplants, sliced thinly

Salt and freshly ground pepper

8 potatoes, peeled and diced

1/2 cup olive oil

2 large onions, chopped coarsely

4 cloves garlic, chopped

1 red bell pepper, seeded and sliced thinly

2 green bell peppers, seeded and sliced thinly

1/2 cup fresh parsley, chopped finely

8–10 tomatoes, seeded and sliced

2 teaspoons paprika

Vinegar

Swiss Chard and Mushroom Lasagna

Makes 4–6 servings

1¹/₂ pounds Swiss chard, chopped coarsely
(including the stems)

5 tablespoons olive oil

1 large white onion, chopped coarsely

2¹/₂ cups sliced mushrooms

1 clove garlic, minced

1 egg

32 ounces low-fat ricotta cheese

2 teaspoons fresh thyme

1 cup fresh basil leaves, chopped

Salt and freshly ground pepper

16 lasagna noodles

3¹/₂ cups homemade or prepared Tomato
Sauce (page 212)

1 Preheat the oven to 350°F. Boil the chard in salted water for 15–20 minutes, until tender. Drain. Pour 3 tablespoons of the olive oil into a large skillet and sauté the onion over medium heat for 2–3 minutes, until golden. Mix the chard and onions together and set aside.

2 Pour the remaining 2 tablespoons of oil into a nonstick saucepan and add the mushrooms and garlic. Sauté over medium-low heat for 2–3 minutes.

3 Beat the egg in a deep bowl, add the ricotta, thyme, basil, and salt and pepper, and mix well. Add the mushrooms and mix well.

4 Boil the lasagna noodles in salted water for about 2 minutes, maximum (they must be al dente). Drain.

5 Pour 1¹/₂ cups of tomato sauce into the bottom of a 9-inch square baking dish. Arrange 4 lasagna noodles over the sauce. Top with a thin layer of the chard mixture and finish with a thin layer of the mushroom mixture. Top with 4 more noodles and 1 cup tomato sauce, and repeat the two-step procedure, ending with a layer of noodles and sauce. Cover with foil and bake for about 40 minutes. Remove the foil and continue baking for another 10–15 minutes. Remove from the oven and serve hot.

Deviled Egg
Casserole

1 Preheat the oven to 375°F. Cook the noodles in salted boiling water according to the instructions in the package. Cook the spinach the same way in a separate pot. When cooked, drain and mix together the noodles and spinach. Place in a well-buttered elongated baking dish and level the surface.

2 Melt the butter in a separate pot and gradually stir the milk and cheese into it. Stir continually over medium-low heat until a creamy sauce is formed.

3 Slice the eggs in half lengthwise and remove the yolks. Place the yolks in a deep bowl and add the garlic, parsley, mustard, Worcestershire sauce, milk, and salt and pepper. Mash and mix well.

4 Fill in egg whites with the yolk mixture. Arrange the eggs, filling side up, on the noodle mixture. Pour the cheese sauce over it, making sure the top surface is covered evenly. Sprinkle the Parmesan cheese over the whole top.

5 Bake for 30–40 minutes, until the top turns golden brown. Remove the casserole from the oven, allow it to rest and cool for 2 or 3 minutes, then serve.

Makes 6 servings

1 (16-ounce) package egg noodles

1/2 pound fresh or frozen spinach, washed well if fresh

8 tablespoons (1 stick) butter or margarine

2 cups milk

1/2 cup grated mozzarella cheese

6 hard-boiled eggs, peeled

2 cloves garlic, minced

3 tablespoons fresh parsley, chopped finely

2 tablespoons French mustard

2 tablespoons Worcestershire sauce

3 tablespoons milk or cream

Salt and freshly ground pepper

Grated Parmesan cheese

Gratin
Dauphinois

1 Preheat the oven to 275°F. Arrange the potatoes in slightly overlapping layers in an 8-cup gratin or baking dish. Mix together with milk and cream in a bowl, then pour over the potatoes to just cover. Bake for 1 hour.

2 Remove from the oven and generously season the top of potatoes with salt and pepper and nutmeg. Return the pan to the oven and bake for 1–1^1/$_2$ hours more, until the liquid is thick and bubbling and the top is golden brown.

Makes 6 servings

2 pounds large russet potatoes, peeled and
   sliced thinly
1^1/$_4$ cups whole milk
1^1/$_4$ cups heavy cream
Salt and freshly ground pepper
Freshly grated nutmeg

Eggplant
Tian

Makes 6 servings

4 medium eggplants, trimmed and sliced
    thinly lengthwise
Salt
4 eggs
Bread crumbs
Vegetable oil, for frying
32 ounces tomato sauce
3 tablespoons dried thyme
6 leaves chopped basil
4 cloves garlic, minced
Freshly ground pepper
Grated Parmesan cheese

1 Preheat the oven to 350°F. Spread out the eggplant slices in a large, flat dish. Sprinkle with salt and set aside for at least 1 hour.

2 Beat the eggs in a deep bowl and spread the bread crumbs on a flat plate. Dip each eggplant slice into the beaten eggs, then dip them in the bread crumbs, to coat each side. Pour the oil into a large nonstick skillet, filling to about a half an inch. Heat over medium-high heat. When the oil is hot, fry the eggplant, flipping to fry both sides until golden brown. As they are cooked, transfer them to a dish lined with paper towels, to drain.

3 While the eggplants are frying, pour the tomato sauce into a saucepan and add the herbs, garlic, and pepper. Cook for for 8–10 minutes over medium-low heat, then turn off the heat.

4 Generously butter 13 × 9-inch ovenproof dish. Cover the bottom of the dish with one-third of the eggplant slices, then cover the eggplant with one-third of the tomato sauce. Sprinkle one-third of the grated cheese evenly on top. Repeat the layers two more times.

5 Pour the remaining beaten eggs over the top surface and spread evenly with a spatula. Bake for about 30 minutes. When the *tian* is done, allow it to cool for 2 or 3 minutes before serving.

Swiss Chard Tian

Makes 4–6 servings

1 pound Swiss chard, trimmed and chopped
    (including the stems)
4 tablespoons olive oil
1 onion, chopped coarsely
3 cloves garlic, minced
3 eggs
Salt and freshly ground pepper
4 teaspoons water
Bread crumbs

1 Preheat the oven to 350°F. Boil the chard in lightly salted water for about 20 minutes. Drain and set aside.

2 Pour the olive oil into a large skillet. Add the onion and sauté lightly over medium-low heat for 2–3 minutes. Add the garlic and sauté for another minute. Add the Swiss chard and continue to sauté for 2–3 more minutes, stirring.

3 Beat the eggs in a deep bowl and add the salt and pepper and the water. Mix well.

4 Generously butter an 11 × 7-inch ovenproof dish. Place the chard mixture into it and spread evenly. Pour the egg mixture on the top and also spread evenly. Sprinkle bread crumbs evenly over the top. Bake for 25–30 minutes. Serve hot.

Zucchini
Tian

Makes 6 servings

10 tablespoons olive oil, divided

1 large zucchini, cut into 3/4-inch slices

2 large Spanish onions, chopped

1 cup uncooked white rice

Salt and freshly ground pepper

1 teaspoon dried thyme

2 cups water

4 eggs

1/2 cup milk

Bread crumbs

1 Preheat the oven to 350°F. Pour oil into a large skillet, heat over medium-high heat, and fry both sides of the zucchini slices. The slices must remain firm, so do not over-fry. As they get done, place them on a dish lined with paper towels, to drain. Set aside.

2 Next, pour more oil into the skillet and sauté the onions for 3–4 minutes over medium-low heat, until they begin to wilt. Set aside.

3 Meanwhile, place the rice in a saucepan, add 2 teaspoons of oil, and mix well. Add salt and pepper and the thyme. Add the water, stir a few times, cover, and then cook the rice over medium-low heat for approximately 20–30 minutes. When the rice is done, turn off the heat.

4 Beat the eggs thoroughly in a deep bowl, add the milk and a pinch each of salt and pepper, and beat again.

5 Generously butter a 10 × 10 × 2-inch ovenproof dish. Cover the bottom of the dish with half of the zucchini slices, then cover them with half of the onion mixture, topped with half of the rice mixture. Repeat the layers once more with the remaining zucchini, onion, and rice.

6 Pour the egg mixture evenly over the top surface and allow it to reach the bottom of the dish. Allow the dish to rest for 10 minutes, then spread the bread crumbs over the top surface. Bake for about 30 minutes. When the *tian* is done, allow it to cool for about 3 minutes before serving.

Rice and Pasta

*R*ice is a wonderful grain, one of the most popular in all the world's cuisines and also one of the most nutritious. I often enjoy preparing rice in the monastery. It is such an easy, versatile, and gentle staple to handle. Rice is also rich in iron, zinc, vitamin B, and plenty of folic acid, which our body needs daily to turn into much-needed energy. From a cultural point of view, rice has always been an integral part of the basic Mediterranean diet, and thus of the diet of Christian monasteries in that part of the world, just as much as it has always been part of the diet of Buddhist monks in Japan, China, Korea, and the rest of the Orient.

Many food historians claim that rice was first introduced to southern Europe—France, Spain, and Italy—by the Saracens, the Muslim population that invaded that region of Europe. In Italy the humble staple received the name *risotto*, whereas in France it was called *riz* and in Spain it became known as *arroz*. In those countries, rice is held in high esteem to this day, which means it is always served separately and not as a side dish, as is often the custom in the United States. In general, I consider rice to be such a handy and versatile grain that it can easily accompany and variety of meat, seafood, vegetable, or egg dishes. When caught in a last-minute dilemma as what to serve with a particular vegetable or fish, I always reach for a cup of rice. I know in advance the result shall always be agreeable to both the eyes and the palate. In the monastery kitchen, rice is always in season.

When it comes to choosing a particular type of rice for a meal, I must honestly confess that I use all different brands and varieties in our daily cooking. I do, however, have a certain predilection for arborio rice, which is de rigueur in Italian dishes that require the staple. The lovely thing about arborio rice is its creamy texture while at the same time the rice is firm and al dente. Like pasta, rice should never be overcooked and served mushy, neither it should be smothered with a heavy sauce. In all instances, the rice presented at the table must always preserve its delicate and intricate texture as well as its subtle and delightful flavor. A few herbs, such as thyme or rosemary or laurel (bay leaf), or a touch of garlic, onion, or grated cheese, suffice to enhance the flavor of this wonderful staple.

The historical background of pasta, or "food of the blessed," as some like to call it, is dotted with insightful and amusing legends about its origins in the Italian kitchen. There are as many stories concocted about pasta's birthplace as there are varied and distinct geographical regions in Italy.

One of these legends likes to tell how the Venetian traveler Marco Polo (ca. 1254–1324) brought noodles back to Venice from a trip he once made to China. Recent research, however, shows that Italians had been eating pasta for at least a few centuries before Marco Polo's expedition.

It is likely that pasta, in one form or another, existed from time immemorial and it simply got reinvented each time it was

---

Pasta is no longer considered just a *primo piatto*, a first course. It can be a quick and satisfying lunch as well as the focus of an artful and sophisticated dinner . . . Pasta has come to symbolize all that is fresh and spontaneous about the way we eat today. It is more than just an ethnic food set apart from everyday eating. It is embraced by everyone for its comforting qualities, easy preparations, healthfulness, and magical ability to tap into our communal and individual fantasy of Italy.

—Viana La Place and Evan Kleinman, *Pasta Fresca*

discovered again and again by the other regions of Italy or even outside Italy by other countries.

From Italy, pasta has proliferated all over the world. This was due in grand part to the Italian immigrations of the nineteenth and twentieth centuries. Today, pasta is found even in the remotest corners of the planet. In our American supermarkets, one is often baffled by the immense variety and quality of the pastas offered, as also by the shapes and sizes. And no matter how many varieties one may encounter at the store, they represent only a small percentage of the many types one finds in Italy and throughout the world. It is a fact that pasta has become a daily staple, not only in Italy, but throughout the entire planet. One often wonders, Why so many varieties of pasta? Well, if you live in Italy, for example, you will hear the Italians swear that each type of pasta tastes different from the others. The way and speed a certain type of pasta dries or thickens; whether it is homemade or store-bought; whether it is baked, boiled, or stuffed; the way a certain pasta blends with the sauce, etc., are all recognized by the Italians, experts as they are in daily pasta consumption. The Italians, throughout the centuries, have perfected the art of pasta preparation with their ever-delightful imagination and love of good food. When it comes to pasta, their palates are as refined as their appetites are insatiable.

When choosing to serve pasta for dinner, some considerations may be helpful. One is to pay attention to the size and type of pasta chosen for the occasion; the nutrients contained in that particular type of pasta, such as whether it is rich in vitamin B, iron, and/or calcium; whether it is made from cheap flour versus good semolina, or even whole wheat. Some types of pasta also add to their preparation spinach, squash, or other vegetables, for color and flavor. The other important point to make here, directly related to pasta preparation, is not to overcook the noodles, but to prepare them al dente, as do the Italians. Italians happen to love the texture and subtle flavor of their pastas, therefore they never overcook them or serve them mushy, as sometimes is done here. On the contrary, by cooking the pasta al dente, they seek to preserve and enhance their pasta's freshness, texture, and individual qualities. It is this respect on the part of the Italians for the ingredients and the quality of pasta they produce that captivates the rest of us as we learn to prepare and eat pasta *alla italiana*.

In Italian cuisine, pasta is often served with a delicate sauce—tomato, pesto, or another concoction of vegetables, herbs, meat, or seafood. The sauces are never overwhelming and they are served only in small amounts and right proportion. They are never intended to drown the pasta or submerge them in a liquid bath. In most cases, the sauce is there simply to blend gently and lightly with the pasta, preserving and enhancing at all costs the fine individual pasta texture and originality.

Rice is a beautiful food. It is beautiful when it grows, precision rows of sparkling green stalks shooting up to reach the hot summer sun. It is beautiful when harvested, autumn gold sheaves piled on diked, patchwork paddies. It is beautiful when, once threshed, it enters granary bins like a flood of tiny seed-pearls. It is beautiful when cooked by a practiced hand, pure white and sweetly fragrant.

—Shizuo Tsuji

Flavorful Risotto from Campania

1 Place the onion and garlic in a large saucepan. Add the parsley, thyme, and olive oil. Cook slowly over medium-low heat, stirring constantly, allowing the onion, garlic, and herbs to sweat until they turn soft. (Don't let the onions brown.) Add the rice to the saucepan and mix it well with the onion mixture. Add salt and pepper. Keep stirring until the rice begins to change color. Pour in the wine and stir some more.

2 When the rice has been absorbed by the wine, add about half of the tomatoes to the saucepan and mix well. Continue to cook the rice, still stirring. (This continual stirring is part of the process of preparing a good risotto.) After the rice absorbs the liquid from the first batch of tomatoes, add the remaining tomatoes, and also add the boiling water slowly as needed, continuing to stir, until all the liquid is absorbed by the rice.

3 Once the risotto is cooked yet still al dente, add the grated cheese and mix well. Remove from the heat, cover, and let stand to absorb the cheese for about 10 minutes before serving. Serve hot.

Makes 6 servings

1 medium white onion, chopped finely

2 cloves garlic, minced

$^1/_3$ cup flat-leaf Italian parsley, chopped finely

2 tablespoons fresh or 1 tablespoon dried thyme

5 tablespoons good-quality virgin olive oil

2 cups arborio rice

Salt and freshly ground pepper

$^1/_2$ cup dry white wine

$1^1/_2$ cups fresh tomatoes, peeled, seeded, and finely chopped

1 cup boiling water

$^1/_3$ cup grated pecorino or Parmigiano-Reggiano cheese

Mushroom–
Wild Rice Pilaf

Makes 4–6 servings

1 Pour the olive oil into a nonstick pot, add the onion and, mushrooms, and sauté lightly over medium-low heat until the vegetables soften. Add the garlic and lemon zest, and stir well for about 1 minute.

2 At this point, add the rice, stock, and salt and pepper, and over medium heat bring to a rapid boil. Lower the heat to medium-low, stir the rice, cover, and simmer slowly until all the liquid is absorbed, 30–40 minutes.

3 When the rice is done, check the seasonings and serve immediately, sprinkled with chervil.

6 tablespoons olive oil

1 onion, chopped finely

8 mushrooms, sliced thinly

2 clove garlic, minced finely

Zest of 1 lemon, minced finely

1 1/2 cup uncooked wild rice

3 cups vegetable stock or water

Salt and freshly ground pepper

Finely chopped fresh chervil, for garnish

1 In a large nonstick saucepan, heat the oil over medium-low heat and sauté the onion. When the onion begins to turn golden, add the garlic and mushrooms. Mix well.

2 While sautéing the onion, in a separate pot bring the vegetable stock to a boil. Add the wine. Lower the heat to a gentle simmer.

3 Add the rice to the onion mixture and make sure the rice is well coated. Stirring continually, add 1 cup of the simmering stock mixture and raise the heat beneath the rice pot to medium. Continue to stir until almost all the liquid is absorbed.

4 While stirring, add the chickpeas and 1 more cup of the stock. Continue to stir for another 4 or 5 minutes, adding more of the stock mixture as needed. The rice must be kept moist at all times.

5 Add the spinach and continue to add the remainder of the stock mixture gradually, while continuing to stir. Before adding the last cup of stock, add salt and pepper to taste. Keep stirring until all the liquid is absorbed, and check the seasonings.

6 Remove the saucepan from the heat, add the cheese, and stir gently a few times. Cover the saucepan and set aside for about 5 minutes before serving. Serve hot.

Chickpea and Spinach Risotto

Makes 4 servings

5 tablespoons olive oil

1 onion, chopped finely

2 cloves garlic, minced

4 baby bella mushrooms, chopped finely

4 cups vegetable stock or water

1 cup dry white wine

1 cup uncooked arborio rice

$1/2$ cup canned chickpeas, drained and rinsed

2 cups well-washed spinach, finely chopped

Salt and freshly ground pepper

$1/3$ cup Parmesan or Romano cheese, grated

Parsnip Risotto

Makes 6 servings

8 cups vegetable stock
5 tablespoons butter
2 cups chopped onion
1 1/2 pounds parsnips (about 7 medium), peeled, trimmed, and cut into 1/4-inch pieces
5 teaspoons chopped fresh rosemary
1 1/2 cups (10 ounces) arborio rice
3/4 cup freshly grated Parmesan cheese

1 Bring the stock to a boil in a medium saucepan over high heat. Lower the heat to low, cover, and keep warm.

2 Melt 4 tablespoons of the butter in large, heavy saucepan over medium heat. Add the onion and cook until tender, stirring often, about 10 minutes. Stir in the parsnips and 3 teaspoons of the chopped rosemary. Cook until the parsnips begin to brown, stirring occasionally, 7–8 minutes.

3 Add the rice and, stirring constantly, cook for 2 minutes. Add enough warm stock to cover; simmer until almost all stock is absorbed, stirring occasionally, about 5 minutes. Add more stock, 1 cup at a time, and cook until the rice and parsnips are tender, allowing each addition of stock to be absorbed before more is added, and stirring frequently.

4 Remove from the heat; stir in the remaining 1 tablespoon of butter, the remaining 2 teaspoons of rosemary, and the cheese. Season the risotto to taste with salt and pepper. Divide among six shallow bowls and serve.

Rice-Herb-Cheese Croquettes

Makes 6–8 servings

2 cups arborio rice

4 cups water

Salt

1 tablespoon butter

4 eggs

Freshly ground pepper

1 teaspoon dried or 3 teaspoons fresh thyme

2 teaspoons dried or 5 teaspoons fresh chives

4 tablespoons dried or 7 tablespoons fresh
    parsley, chopped finely if fresh

1 teaspoon dried oregano

1 1/4 cups dry bread crumbs

1/2 cup grated Gruyère cheese, or your
    preferred cheese, such as Parmesan
    or Romano

Vegetable or olive oil, for deep frying

1 Place the rice in a large saucepan. Add the water and a pinch of salt and bring to a boil. Cook over medium-low heat until all the liquid is absorbed, approximately 40 minutes, then add the butter and mix well. Transfer the rice to a dish and allow it to cool

2 Break the eggs into a deep bowl. Add salt and pepper and beat with a whisk or a mixer. Add all the herbs and mix well with a fork.

3 Add the rice, 3/4 cup of the bread crumbs, and the cheese to the egg mixture and mix well. Set aside for 1 hour at room temperature.

4 Preheat the oven to 250°F. Moisten your hands with water and shape the rice mixture into 2-inch croquettes by rolling them carefully into balls with both hands. Spread the remaining 1/2 cup of bread crumbs in a flat dish and roll the croquettes in the crumbs to coat.

5 Line a dish with paper towels. Pour the oil into a deep, nonstick skillet and heat over high heat. Fry the croquettes in small batches at a time, taking care to turn them so all sides are equally cooked and browned. When the croquettes are done, transfer them one by one to the lined dish, to drain. Transfer the croquettes to an ovenproof dish and warm them in a 250°F oven until ready to serve. Serve hot.

Rice Tortillitas

1 Preheat the oven to 250°F. In a deep bowl, mix the eggs with a whisk or mixer. Add the milk and mix some more.

2 Add the cooked rice, cheese, shallots, parsley, and salt and pepper to taste. Mix well with a fork.

3 Pour the oil into a large, deep skillet and heat it over medium-high heat. When the oil is hot, add the rice by rounded spoonfuls, leaving space between them. When one side is done, turn rounds over with a spatula and cook the other side. As the *tortillitas* get done, drain them on paper towels before transferring them to an ovenproof dish. Keep them warm in the oven until ready to serve. They make wonderful appetizers before dinner.

Makes 4–6 servings

4 eggs
1 1/2 cups milk
3/4 cup cooked rice
1/3 cup Parmigiano-Reggiano cheese, grated
2 shallots, minced finely
A few sprigs parsley, chopped finely
Salt and freshly ground pepper
Olive or vegetable oil, for deep frying

Mediterranean Paella

1 Heat the oil in a heavy, preferably cast-iron, saucepan. Add the onion, tomato, and garlic, and sauté over low heat for 1–2 minutes, stirring frequently.

2 Add the peppers, peas, olives, capers, and mushrooms. Continue to sauté for another 2 minutes. Add the rice, paprika, and saffron and, stirring continually, cook for 1–2 minutes, until the rice begins to change color.

3 Pour in the boiling stock and raise the heat to medium. (You may wish to add a bit more water, if necessary, or even ¹/₂ cup of dry white wine on festive occasions.) Add salt and pepper. Stirring frequently, cook over medium heat for about 15 minutes, then lower the heat to medium-low and continue to cook until the rice is al dente. Once the rice is cooked, cover, turn off the heat, and let the rice rest for 3–4 minutes before serving.

Makes 6 servings

8 tablespoons olive oil, plus additional
    if needed

1 onion, chopped finely

1 tomato, peeled, seeded, and chopped

3 cloves garlic, minced

2 red bell peppers, roasted, peeled, then
    seeded and chopped

¹/₂ cup shelled fresh peas

12 pitted green olives, chopped

¹/₃ cup capers

12 mushrooms, trimmed and sliced in half

2 cups uncooked arborio rice

1 teaspoon paprika

A pinch saffron

6 cups boiling vegetable stock or water

Salt and freshly ground pepper

Linguine in Spicy Sauce

Makes 6–8 servings

1 Prepare the sauce by heating $^1/_3$ cup of olive oil in a medium pot. Add the onion, tomatoes, garlic, chile pepper, basil, and salt. Cook over medium heat for 15–20 minutes, stirring often.

2 Bring lightly salted water to a boil in a large saucepan. Add the linguine and 2 tablespoons of oil, and cook for 5–8 minutes. The linguine must remain al dente. Drain.

3 Mix the pasta and the sauce well. Serve hot and offer a bowl of grated cheese at the table to pass around.

$^1/_3$ cup plus 2 tablespoons olive oil

1 onion, chopped coarsely

10 plum tomatoes, peeled, seeded, and chopped

4 cloves garlic, minced

1 small dried chile pepper, crumbled

$^1/_4$ cup fresh basil leaves, chopped finely

Salt

1 pound uncooked linguine

Grated Parmesan or Romano cheese

1 About 30 minutes before serving, place the arugula and parsley in a food processor. Add the yogurt, goat cheese, and salt and pepper to taste. Blend thoroughly. Keep the sauce at room temperature until ready to use.

2 Bring lightly salted water to a boil in a large saucepan. Cook the pasta in the boiling water, following the instructions on the package. Drain and divide among four serving dishes. Pour the sauce evenly over each serving and serve immediately, sprinkled with Parmesan cheese.

Pasta with Arugula and Goat Cheese

Makes 4 servings

1 bunch fresh arugula, chopped

4 sprigs parsley, chopped

1 (18-ounce) container low-fat yogurt or
   sour cream

$1/3$ cup goat cheese, crumbled

Salt and freshly ground pepper

1 pound uncooked fusilli pasta

Grated Parmesan cheese, for garnish

Lemon-Scented Spaghetti

1 fennel bulb, sliced thinly
1 pound uncooked spaghetti
$1/3$ cup plus 1 tablespoon olive oil
20 pitted black olives
4 cloves garlic, peeled
$1/4$ cup lemon juice
1 teaspoon lemon zest, grated or finely diced
A few sprigs parsley, chopped
Salt and freshly ground pepper
Grated cheese (optional)

1 Bring lightly salted water to boil in a large saucepan. Add the fennel, spaghetti, and 1 tablespoon of olive oil. Cook according to the instructions on the spaghetti package. The pasta must remain al dente. Drain.

2 Meanwhile, prepare the sauce by placing the olives, garlic, lemon juice, lemon zest, and parsley in a small food processor. Blend well.

3 Heat $1/3$ cup of olive oil in a large, deep, heavy-based pan. Add the olive mixture and sauté for a minute or two over medium-low heat, stirring constantly. Add the spaghetti mixture and salt and pepper, and mix with care until the pasta is coated evenly with the sauce. Serve hot and, if you wish, offer a bowl of finely grated cheese at the table to pass around.

Linguine di Parma

Makes 6 servings

1 pound uncooked linguine

3 tablespoons butter

16 asparagus spears, trimmed and sliced into
    2-inch lengths

4 tablespoons fresh parsley, chopped finely

3 tablespoons fresh basil, chopped finely

$2/3$ cup heavy cream

Salt and freshly ground pepper

$1/3$ cup Parmesan cheese, grated

1 Bring lightly salted water to a boil in a large saucepan. Add the linguine. Cook according to the instructions on the linguine package. The pasta must remain al dente. Drain and place back in the pot.

2 Meanwhile heat the butter in a large non-stick skillet, add the asparagus, and sauté over medium heat for about 3 minutes, stirring frequently.

3 Add the parsley, basil, heavy cream, and salt and pepper. Cook, stirring continually, for 2–3 minutes. Add the grated cheese and mix well.

4 When ready to serve, pour the asparagus mixture into the saucepan containing the linguine and toss gently, making sure the pasta is well coated with the sauce. Serve hot, accompanied by a bowl of grated cheese for those who wish to add a bit more.

Farfalle Piamontese

1 Bring lightly salted water to a boil in a large saucepan. Add the farfalle, arugula, and 1 tablespoon of olive oil. Cook according to the instructions on the farfalle package. The pasta must remain al dente. Drain.

2 Pour 1/3 cup of oil into a large nonstick skillet, add the zucchini, and sauté for 4–5 minutes over medium-low heat, stirring frequently. Just before serving, add the cherry tomatoes, garlic, oregano, and salt and pepper, and sauté for only 1 minute. Be careful to keep the tomatoes intact.

3 Mix the pasta with the sauce. (Toss carefully because of the tomatoes.) Serve hot, sprinkled with grated cheese.

Makes 4–6 servings

1 pound uncooked farfalle (butterfly) pasta

1 bunch fresh arugula, trimmed

1/3 cup plus 1 tablespoon extra-virgin olive oil

2 medium zucchini, sliced thinly

1 cup red cherry tomatoes, seeded and sliced in half

1 cup yellow cherry tomatoes, seeded and sliced in half

2 cloves garlic, minced

1 teaspoon dried or 3 teaspoons fresh oregano

Salt and freshly ground pepper

Grated Pecorino Romano cheese

Tagliatelle with Chickpeas Tuscan Style

1 Pour 4 tablespoons of olive oil into a large, deep, heavy-based skillet and heat over medium-low heat. Add the onion and cook until soft, stirring from time to time. Add the garlic, bouquet garni, and tomatoes. Cook for about 3 minutes, stirring often. Add the chickpeas and bring to a simmer. Add salt and pepper to taste. Lower the heat to low, stir well one more time, cover the skillet, and allow the sauce to simmer gently for about 20 minutes, stirring occasionally. When the sauce is done, remove and discard the bouquet garni.

2 Bring lightly salted water to a boil in a large saucepan. Add the tagliatelle and 1 teaspoon of olive oil. Cook according to the instructions on the tagliatelle package. The pasta must remain al dente. Drain. Drizzle the remaining 2 tablespoons of olive oil over the tagliatelle and stir gently. Divide the tagliatelle among six serving dishes. Spoon the sauce over the pasta. Sprinkle some grated Parmesan over the top and serve hot.

Makes 6 servings

6 tablespoons plus 1 teaspoon extra-virgin
   olive oil
1 onion, chopped
4 cloves garlic, minced finely
1 bouquet garni (1 sprig each basil, rosemary,
   and thyme, and 1 bay leaf tied together
   in a square of cheesecloth, or the
   equivalent in dried herbs if fresh ones
   are not available)
3 medium tomatoes, peeled, seeded, and
   coarsely chopped
1 (15-ounce) can chickpeas, drained
Salt and freshly ground pepper
1 pound good-quality tagliatelle, fresh
   if possible
Grated Parmesan cheese

Rotini with Chickpeas

1 Place the chickpeas in a container filled with water. Add the baking soda and soak overnight.

2 The following day, drain and rinse the chickpeas. Place in a saucepan and add water, 3 tablespoons of olive oil, a pinch of salt, and the rosemary. Bring the water to a boil, cover, and lower the heat to medium. Cook for about 3 hours, adding more water if needed, until the chickpeas are tender.

3 Bring again to a boil, add the garlic and rotini, and lower the heat to medium. Cook according to the instructions on the rotini package. The pasta must remain al dente. Drain. Remove the rosemary.

4 Heat the remaining 10 tablespoons of olive oil in a saucepan, add the balsamic vinegar, pasta mixture, parsley, and salt and pepper to taste. Toss gently and make sure that the peas and pasta are well coated with the oil. Serve hot, and offer a bowl of grated cheese at the table to pass around.

Makes 4–6 servings

2 cups dried chickpeas, or 1 (15-ounce) can, drained and rinsed

1 teaspoon baking soda

8 cups water

13 tablespoons extra-virgin olive oil, plus more if needed

Salt

1 sprig rosemary

5 cloves garlic, minced

1 pound uncooked rotini pasta

1 tablespoon balsamic vinegar

1 bunch fresh parsley, chopped finely

Freshly ground pepper

Pecorino or Parmesan cheese, grated

Rigatoni with Eggplant

Makes 6–8 servings

1/3 cup plus 2 tablespoons olive oil
2 medium eggplants, cubed
10 plum tomatoes, peeled, seeded, and
    chopped
1 onion, chopped
3 cloves garlic, minced
1 bay leaf
Several fresh basil leaves, chopped
Salt and freshly ground pepper
1 pound uncooked rigatoni pasta
Grated Romano cheese, for garnish

1 Pour 1/3 cup olive oil into a large nonstick saucepan. Add the vegetables, heat over medium heat, and cook for a few minutes, stirring often. Add the bay leaf, basil, and salt and pepper. Mix well, cover, and lower the heat to medium-low. Cook for about 20 minutes, stirring occasionally. Check the seasonings. Remove the bay leaf when the sauce is done.

2 Meanwhile, bring lightly salted water to a boil in another saucepan. Add 2 tablespoons oil and rigatoni. Cook according to the instructions on the rigatoni package. The pasta must remain al dente. Drain.

3 Mix the pasta and the sauce well, so that the pasta is thoroughly coated with the sauce. Transfer the mixture to a serving dish. Sprinkle the grated cheese on the top. Serve hot, and, if you wish, offer a bowl of grated cheese at the table to pass around.

Fettuccine di Corsica

Makes 4–6 servings

1 pound uncooked fettuccine

7 tablespoons olive oil

3 cloves garlic, minced

3 tomatoes, peeled, seeded, and chopped

1/2 cup pitted black olives, chopped coarsely

6 tablespoons capers

1/24 cup dry white wine

16 fresh basil leaves, chopped finely

1 (2-ounce) can anchovies, drained and finely chopped (optional)

Salt and freshly ground pepper (optional)

Grated Romano cheese (optional)

1 Bring lightly salted water to a boil in a large saucepan. Add the fettuccine and 2 tablespoons of olive oil. Cook according to the instructions on the fettuccine package. The pasta must remain al dente. Drain.

2 In the meantime, pour the remaining 5 tablespoons of olive oil into a large nonstick skillet and add the garlic. Sauté for 1 minute over medium-low heat, stirring continually. Add the tomatoes, olives, and capers. Continue to sauté for another 3 minutes, stirring often.

3 When the tomatoes begin to wilt and turn into a sauce, add the wine, basil, anchovies, and salt and pepper. Stir, cover the skillet, and continue to cook for another 5–6 minutes.

4 Drain the fettuccine and return it to the saucepan. Pour the sauce over it and toss gently, making sure all the noodles get coated and the sauce is evenly distributed. Serve hot, and offer a bowl of grated cheese at the table to pass around.

Gnocchi with Arugula and Watercress

1 Bring lightly salted water to a boil in a large saucepan. Add the gnocchi and 1 tablespoon of the oil. Cook over medium heat, following the directions on the gnocchi package. Halfway through the cooking, add half of the arugula and half of the watercress. When cooked, drain and keep the gnocchi covered.

2 Rub the crushed garlic thoroughly into a large nonstick skillet, and then discard it. Pour the remaining 6 tablespoons of olive oil into the skillet and heat it. Add the remaining arugula and watercress and sauté lightly over medium-low heat for a few minutes, until they wilt. Add the gnocchi and ground pepper and toss gently until all is well mixed. Divide the gnocchi among four serving dishes plates, top with grated cheese. Serve hot, and, if you wish, offer a bowl of grated cheese at the table to pass around.

Makes 4 servings

1 (14-ounce) package frozen gnocchi

7 tablespoons virgin olive oil

1 bunch fresh arugula, trimmed

1 bunch fresh watercress, trimmed

1 clove garlic, crushed

Freshly ground pepper

Romano Pecorino cheese, grated

Gnocchi with Mushrooms and Zucchini

Makes 4 servings

1 (14-ounce) package frozen gnocchi

4 tablespoons olive oil

4 tablespoons butter

16 mushrooms, cleaned, trimmed, and sliced
  in half

2 small to medium zucchini, quartered
  lengthwise, then cut into small pieces

2 shallots, or 1 small Vidalia onion, chopped

2 cloves garlic, minced

2 tablespoons water

$1/3$ cup dry white wine

Finely chopped fresh parsley

Salt and freshly ground pepper

Romano cheese, grated

1 Bring lightly sated water to a boil in a large saucepan. Add the gnocchi and 1 tablespoon of the olive oil. Cook over medium heat, following the directions on the gnocchi package, usually about 3 minutes. Drain and keep covered.

2 Melt the butter in a large nonstick skillet, and add the mushrooms and zucchini. Cook over low heat for about 4 minutes, stirring often. Add the shallots, garlic, the remaining 3 tablespoons of olive oil, and the water. Mix well and continue to cook for another minute. Add the wine, parsley, and salt and pepper. Mix well and continue to cook for another 2 minutes. Add the gnocchi. Mix well, cover the skillet, and cook for 2–3 minutes. Turn off the heat.

3 Sprinkle with grated cheese and serve immediately.

Acorn Squash–Mushroom Lasagna

1 Preheat the oven to 350°F. Melt the butter in large skillet over medium-high heat. Add the onion and sauté until soft, about 8 minutes. Raise the heat to high, add the mushrooms, and cook until tender, stirring constantly, about 3 minutes. Season with salt and pepper. Transfer to a bowl and set aside.

2 Place in same skillet the squash, stock, and 3 tablespoons each of the thyme and sage. Cover and simmer over medium heat for 10 minutes, or until the squash is just tender. Uncover and cook until squash is very soft but still retains its shape, about 5 more minutes. Season with salt and pepper.

3 Mix the ricotta, 2 cups of the mozzarella cheese, 1^1/2 cups of the Parmesan, and the remaining 1 tablespoon each of thyme and sage in large bowl. Season to taste with salt and pepper; mix in eggs.

4 Brush a 13 × 9 × 2-inch glass baking dish with the oil. Spread 1 cup of the ricotta mixture over the bottom. Arrange three noodles on top. Spread 1^1/4 cups of the ricotta mixture over the noodles. Arrange 1^1/3 cups of the squash mixture over that, and sprinkle with half the mushrooms and 1 cup of the remaining mozzarella. Top with three noodles, then with 1^3/4 cups ricotta of the mixture, the remaining squash, and the remaining mushrooms. Top with three noodles. Spread remaining ricotta mixture on top and sprinkle with the remaining ^{1}/2 cup Parmesan. Cover with oiled foil.

5 Bake the lasagna, covered, for 35 minutes. Uncover and bake until heated through, about 25 minutes. Let stand for 10 minutes before serving.

Makes 8 servings

4 tablespoons (^{1}/2 stick) butter

2 cups chopped onions

^{1}/2 pound mushrooms, sliced (about 3 cups)

Salt and freshly ground pepper

2 pounds acorn squash, peeled, seeded, and cut into ^{1}/4-inch-thick slices (about 5^1/2 cups)

1 (14-ounce) can vegetable stock

4 tablespoons chopped fresh thyme

4 tablespoons chopped fresh sage

3 (15-ounce) containers whole-milk ricotta cheese

4 cups grated mozzarella cheese

2 cups grated Parmesan cheese

3 large eggs

Olive oil, for brushing pan

1 (9-ounce) package no-boil lasagna noodles (or boil and drain regular lasagna noodles, following the package instructions)

Fusilli in Fiery Sauce

Makes 4–6 servings

1 Heat 6 tablespoons of the oil in a large nonstick saucepan. Add the garlic, sauté it alone for 30 seconds, then add the tomatoes, onion, and chiles, and cook over medium heat for 12–15 minutes, stirring often, until the tomatoes turn into a sauce.

2 Add the cumin, basil, parsley, and salt, and continue to cook, stirring, for another 5 minutes or so, over medium-low heat. Check the seasonings and the consistency of the sauce. It should be smooth and fiery.

3 Meanwhile, bring lightly salted water to a boil in a large saucepan. Add the fusilli and the remaining 1 tablespoon of olive oil. Cook according to the instructions on the fusilli package. The pasta must remain al dente. Drain.

4 Transfer the pasta into the saucepan with the sauce. Mix well, and serve hot, and offer a bowl of grated cheese at the table to pass around.

7 tablespoons virgin olive oil

4 cloves garlic minced

10 plum tomatoes, peeled, or 10 canned, seeded, and chopped

1 large onion, chopped

2 red chile peppers, seeded and minced

1 teaspoon ground cumin

12 fresh basil leaves, chopped coarsely

A few sprigs flat-leaf Italian parsley, minced

Salt

14 ounces fusilli pasta

Grated Parmesan cheese

Couscous with Portobello Mushrooms

Makes 4–6 servings

4 tablespoons olive oil

4 shallots, trimmed and sliced thinly

8 portobello mushrooms, cleaned and
    sliced thinly

2 cups vegetable stock or water

1 cup uncooked couscous

Salt and freshly ground white pepper

1 Heat the oil in a nonstick casserole and sauté the shallots over medium-low heat for about 2 minutes, stirring continually.

2 Add the mushrooms and continue to cook for about another 3 minutes, until the mushrooms soften.

3 Add the vegetable stock and bring to a boil. Add the couscous and salt and pepper, and, stirring continually, cook for 2 or 3 minutes. Turn off the heat, cover the casserole, and let the couscous stand for 5–6 minutes, until the liquid has been absorbed and the couscous is al dente. Serve hot.

Minted Couscous
(Cold Salad)

Makes 6 servings

1 Bring water to a boil in a large soup pot and add the ears of corn. Boil for 5–6 minutes. Remove the corn and set it aside to cool, then cut the kernels from the cobs, using a sharp knife. Place the corn kernels in a large, deep bowl.

2 Add the cucumbers, celery, and onion to the bowl.

3 Cook the couscous in 2 cups of boiling water for about 3 minutes, stirring continually. Turn off the heat, cover, and let the couscous stand for several minutes until all the water has been absorbed and the couscous is done.

4 Add the couscous to the vegetables in the bowl. Add salt and pepper, mint, cilantro, olive oil, and lemon juice. Toss the ingredients well and chill in the refrigerator for several hours before serving. Serve cold.

NOTE: This is an exciting dish for a summer picnic or a meal outdoors.

6 ears fresh corn, husked

2 medium cucumbers, peeled, seeded, and diced

1 stalk celery, sliced thinly and then diced

1 small Vidalia onion, diced

1 cup uncooked couscous

Salt and freshly ground pepper

1 bunch fresh mint, chopped

1 bunch fresh cilantro, chopped

1/2 cup olive oil

4 teaspoons lemon juice

Part Three

Side Dishes

Vegetables and Mushrooms

Vegetables

ach season has its own significance, both in the garden and in the kitchen, for each season provides its own unique variety in vegetables, some for spring and summer, some for fall and even winter. Throughout the years, living and gardening in the monastery in tune with the seasons has allowed me to serve at our humble table vegetables rich in vitamins, fiber, and nutrients; wonderful in freshness and taste; and exquisite in colors and texture. Once the vegetables are harvested in the garden, they are brought to the kitchen, where, as one can imagine, they are received with delight and treated with the utmost respect. It remains the privilege of the cook to then utilize his culinary talents to create imaginative dishes, full of artfulness and taste, which can later be savored and remembered by the monastic palate and the guests long after the food has been consumed.

Vegetables, a magnificent gift from the Creator, are for everyone. While creating and adapting these recipes for consumption by the public, it never entered my mind that they were to be used by vegetarians and vegans only. On the contrary, these recipes were conceived, first, for each and every person who is interested in a healthy diet; and second, for all those who are tired of presenting vegetables at the table in the same old fashion and are looking for innovative dishes that represent a newer and brighter trend in the kitchen.

The majority of these recipes go well with eggs, seafood, meat, grains, and other dishes. Often they can be served as the main dish or as accompaniment to the main course, as a side dish, or *contorni*, as the Italians would describe them. It is up to the talents and imagination of the chef to adapt and re-create these recipes in meaningful manner, as a delightful surprise for family, friends, or special guests. My hope is that vegetables shall be rediscovered in a new light, be more often in demand, and most of all, become the essential foundation of a cuisine that is as healthy as it is refined.

When selecting vegetables for the table, either in the supermarkets or a farmers' market, choose those that are fresh smelling, firm, brightly colored, crisp, and of good texture. If one is not going to use them in the kitchen on the same day, one must try to preserve them in the refrigerator. For those who are blessed to have a vegetable garden, the best option is to harvest the vegetables the same day they are going to be cooked or eaten, and, whenever possible, just before they are prepared and served. This allows the vegetables to retain not only their freshness and good texture, but more important, all their vitamins and other nutrients.

This is what the Lord Almighty, the God of Israel, says . . . plant gardens and eat what they produce.

—Jeremiah 39:5

From artichokes and asparagus to cabbage and zucchini, there is more interest in fresh vegetables now than ever before. Not only are more varieties available in our supermarkets, but specialty growers and specialty stores are catering to America's increasing demand for superior quality and freshness. In addition, the truth has dawned that fresh vegetables are not only good for you, they are wonderfully good to eat—when lovingly prepared.

—Julia Child, *The Way to Cook*

Roasted Carrots, Parsnips, and Celery

Makes 6–8 servings

5 large carrots, peeled and cut into
    1-inch-thick slices
5 large parsnips, well washed (peeling optional)
    and cut into 1-inch-thick slices
5 stalks celery, washed and cut into
    1-inch lengths
Nonstick vegetable oil spray or regular
    vegetable oil
10 cloves garlic, chopped coarsely
8 tablespoons olive oil
1/2 cup orange juice
Freshly ground pepper
4 tablespoons chopped fresh mint

1 Preheat the oven to 350°F. Place the carrots, parsnips, and celery in a large saucepan in water to cover, bring to a boil, and cook for 2–3 minutes, maximum. Drain under cold water and set aside.

2 Oil a large, deep baking dish. Spread the chopped garlic evenly over the surface. Arrange the blanched vegetables over the garlic. Drizzle with 4 tablespoons of the olive oil and 1/4 cup of the orange juice, and sprinkle with ground pepper and 2 tablespoons of the mint. Repeat to form a second layer. Cover the dish with foil and roast for 25–30 minutes, stirring the vegetables once as they cook and removing the foil during the last 5 minutes of roasting. Remove from the oven and let cool for 4 or 5 minutes. Serve warm or at room temperature as an accompaniment to the main course.

Flageolet Beans à la Dijonnaise

Makes 6–8 servings

1 pound dried flageolet beans, soaked
    overnight
8 cups water
2 carrots, peeled and diced
1 large onion, peeled, left whole, and stuck
    with 4 whole cloves
1 bay leaf
Salt
2 cloves garlic, minced finely
$^1/_3$ cup fresh parsley, chopped finely
$2^1/_2$ tablespoons butter
Freshly ground white pepper

1 Drain and rinse the soaked beans and place in a large casserole. Add the water, carrots, the whole onion studded with cloves, the bay leaf, and salt. Bring the water to a boil, then lower the heat to medium-low and cook, covered, for about 1 hour, stirring occasionally.

2 After about 1 hour, remove the bay leaf and the onion with cloves. Add the garlic, parsley, butter, and pepper. Cover and continue to cook for another 5 minutes. Drain the remaining liquid and serve the beans hot.

Stuffed Tomatoes Biarritz Style

Makes 6 servings

6 medium ripe tomatoes

1 recipe Languedoc Dip (page 23)

5 tablespoons prepared or Mayonnaise
   (page 20)

18 large lettuce leaves

1 Slice the tomatoes horizontally at the very top and carefully scoop out their insides with the help of a pointed spoon.

2 Combine the Languedoc Dip and the Mayonnaise in a small bowl and mix well.

3 When ready to serve, place three lettuce leaves in each plate in the form of a clover leaf, and on the center place a tomato. Fill each tomato with the dip.

NOTE: Serve cold as an appetizer during the summer months, when tomatoes are in season.

Stuffed Red Peppers
Basque Style

Makes 6 servings

1 Preheat the oven to 250°F. Place the pepper halves, hollow side up, in a well-buttered 9 × 9-inch ovenproof dish.

2 Pour the oil into a nonstick skillet. Add the onion and garlic and sauté them lightly for no more than 2 minutes.

3 Place the eggs in a bowl, and add the tuna, parsley, onion mixture, eggs, and salt and pepper. Mix well.

4 Stuff the pepper hollows with the tuna mixture. Sprinkle the tops lightly with bread crumbs. Bake for about 25 minutes. Serve hot.

3 large red bell peppers, sliced in half
    lengthwise and seeded

3 tablespoons olive oil

1 medium onion, chopped

2 cloves garlic, minced

2 hard-boiled eggs, peeled and crumbled

1 (8-ounce) can light tuna fish, crumbled

6 sprigs parsley, chopped finely

2 eggs, beaten

Salt and freshly ground pepper

Bread crumbs

Stuffed **Tomatoes** Bidart

Makes 8 servings

8 medium ripe tomatoes

7 tablespoons olive oil

5 medium onions, chopped

2 medium red bell peppers, seeded and diced

Salt and freshly ground pepper

A few sprigs parsley, chopped finely

Bread crumbs

1 Preheat the oven to 350°F. Slice the tomatoes horizontally at the very top. Carefully scoop out their insides with the help of a pointed spoon, and reserve. Place the tomato shells upside down over a paper towel for about 15 minutes to drain them of their remaining juice.

2 Pour the olive oil into a large skillet or saucepan, add the onions, peppers, about one-third of the reserved tomato flesh, salt and pepper to taste, and parsley. Cook over medium-low heat, stirring occasionally, until the onions begin to soften and a saucelike consistency is achieved.

3 Turn each tomato shell upright and fill with the onion mixture. Place in a well-oiled 11 × 7-inch ovenproof dish. Sprinkle with bread crumbs. Bake for 30 minutes. Serve hot.

Spanish Lima Beans

Makes 4–6 servings

2 pounds fresh or frozen young lima beans

10 tablespoons olive oil

1 large Spanish onion, chopped

1 large red bell pepper, seeded and diced

5 cloves garlic, minced

Salt

1/2 cup water

Freshly ground pepper

3 hard-boiled eggs, peeled and chopped
   coarsely

Finely chopped fresh parsley, for garnish

1 Shell the lima beans and set them aside.

2 Pour the oil into a large nonstick casserole. Add the onion and pepper. Sauté over medium-low heat for 2–3 minutes, until the onions turn lightly golden.

3 Add the garlic, beans, a pinch of salt, and the water. Stir gently, cover, and continue to cook for about 15 minutes, until most of the water is absorbed and the beans are cooked. Drain and discard whatever liquid remains.

4 Place the bean mixture in a serving bowl. Add the pepper, chopped eggs, and parsley. Toss gently and serve.

NOTE: Usually the dish is prepared with ham or bacon. This recipe is my vegetarian version. Meat eaters may add 1 cup of cubed smoked ham, if they wish.

Italian Eggplant Casserole

Makes 4–6 servings

2 medium eggplants, cut lengthwise into
    $^1/_2$-inch slices

Sea salt

Olive oil

2 large Vidalia onions, sliced

2 eggs

2 cups milk

$^1/_3$ cup all-purpose flour

Salt and freshly ground pepper

1 loaf Italian or French bread, cut into
    2-inch slices

Grated Parmesan or Parmigiano-Reggiano
    cheese

1 Preheat the oven to 350°F. Sprinkle both sides of the eggplant slices with the sea salt and set them aside for 1 hour to "sweat."

2 Heat 3 tablespoons olive oil in a large skillet over medium heat. Briefly fry on both sides several slices of the eggplant at a time and transfer them whole to a large plate. Do not overfry; make sure the slices remain firm and whole. Repeat until all the eggplant is fried. Add more oil to the skillet and sauté the onions until they begin to soften. Set aside.

3 Place the eggs, milk, flour, and salt and pepper in a blender and blend until smooth. Set aside.

4 Generously oil an ovenproof dish that is at least 4 inches deep. Cover the bottom of the dish completely with the bread slices, place them tightly right next to each other. Cover the bread evenly with half of the onion mixture. Pour half of the egg mixture over the top. Arrange the eggplant slices tightly on top of the onions to cover the entire surface. Spread the rest of the onions on top of the eggplant, and top with the remaining egg mixture. Sprinkle with grated Parmesan. Bake for 25–30 minutes, until the casserole turns golden and is done. Remove the dish from the oven and allow it to cool and set for a minute or so. Cut into equal slices and serve immediately, while hot.

Baked Tomatoes with Eggs

Makes 6 servings

6 large ripe tomatoes
Salt and freshly ground pepper
A pinch fresh or dried thyme
6 teaspoons parsley, chopped finely
6 large eggs
Virgin olive oil
Grated Romano or Gruyère cheese

1 Preheat the oven to 300°F. Slice the tomatoes horizontally at the very top and save the tops. Carefully scoop out their insides with the help of a pointed spoon, then place upside down over a paper towel for about 15 minutes to drain them of their remaining juice.

2 Sprinkle a bit of salt, pepper, thyme, and 1 teaspoon of the parsley inside each tomato. Carefully break an egg into each tomato. Pour 1 teaspoon of olive oil over each egg. Sprinkle with another pinch of salt and pepper, scatter the grated cheese over the eggs, and replace the tomatoes' respective tops.

3 Brush a baking dish generously with olive oil. Place the tomatoes into the dish, and bake for 25–30 minutes. Serve hot.

1 Soak the beans overnight, then rinse and drain under cold running water.

2 Place the beans and chopped white onion into a large casserole, add plenty of water, tie the thyme, parsley, and bay leaf with kitchen twine to form a bouquet, and add to the beans. Add 1 teaspoon salt and bring the water to a rapid boil. Lower the heat to medium and cook the beans, partially covered and stirring from time to time, for about $1^1/2$ hours, until they are cooked. Drain the beans and remove the bouquet.

3 Meanwhile, melt the butter in a medium nonstick casserole and sauté the yellow onion for 2–3 minutes over medium-low heat. Add the wine, olive oil, tomato sauce, and garlic. Mix well and simmer gently.

4 Add the drained beans to the wine mixture, season with salt and pepper to taste, mix well, and continue to cook the beans, uncovered and stirring from time to time, making sure the beans don't stick at the bottom, until they absorb the liquid. When the beans are done, check the seasonings again and serve hot.

Red Kidney Beans in Wine Sauce

Makes 6 servings

1 pound dried red kidney beans

1 large white onion, chopped

1 sprig thyme

3 sprigs parsley

1 bay leaf

Salt

3 tablespoons unsalted butter

1 large yellow onion, chopped finely

2 cups red wine

$^1/_3$ cup olive oil

1 cup tomato sauce

6 cloves garlic, minced

Freshly ground pepper

Roasted Sweet Potato Wedges

1 Preheat the oven to 400°F.

2 Generously butter an elongated baking pan or dish. Add the sweet potatoes and dot with the butter. Sprinkle with salt and pepper, rosemary, and garlic. Cover the baking pan with foil and place in the center of the oven and bake for 20–25 minutes. Midway through the baking process, gently toss and turn the potatoes over with the help of a spatula; see that both sides are evenly coated with the butter. Serve with care so the slices remain firm and whole.

NOTE: This is a good accompaniment to a fish, egg, or meat course.

Makes 4 servings

6 medium sweet potatoes, sliced into
$^3/_4$-inch chunks

4 tablespoons unsalted butter, cut into
small pieces

Salt and freshly ground pepper

2 teaspoons fresh rosemary, minced

3 cloves garlic, minced

Zucchini
Beignets

Makes 6–8 servings

2 cups all-purpose flour

4 tablespoons cornstarch

1 tablespoon baking powder

Salt and freshly ground white pepper

2 cups cold dark beer

Olive oil, for deep frying

4 medium zucchini, cut into $1/2$-inch slices
   (pat with paper towels to ensure
   they are dry)

1 Prepare the batter in a deep bowl by mixing the flour, cornstarch, baking powder, and salt and pepper. Add the beer and whisk with a mixer until a smooth batter is formed.

2 Pour sufficient oil for deep frying into a large, deep nonstick skillet and heat over medium heat.

3 Line a platter with paper towels. Place about four zucchini slices in the batter at a time and, with the help of tongs, transfer the slices to the hot oil. Cook until they turn golden on both sides, about $1^1/2$ minutes per side. Using clean tongs, remove the cooked beignets to the paper-lined platter to drain. Check the seasonings and serve hot.

1 Place the eggplant slices in a container filled with cold water, add a pinch of salt, and let stand for 2 hours. Drain well, pat dry with paper towels, and set aside.

2 In a deep bowl, prepare the batter by mixing the flour, cornstarch, baking powder, and salt and pepper. Add the beer and whisk with a mixer until a smooth batter is formed.

3 Pour sufficient oil for deep frying into a large, deep nonstick skillet and heat over medium heat.

4 Line a platter with paper towels. Place three eggplant slices in the batter at a time and, with the help of tongs, transfer the slices to the hot oil. Cook until they turn golden on both sides, about 1¹/₂ minutes per side. Using clean tongs, remove the cooked beignets to the paper-lined platter to drain.

Eggplant
Fritters

Makes 6 servings

4 medium eggplants, preferably
   elongated, such as the Japanese type,
   trimmed and cut into ¹/₂-inch slices

Salt

2 cups all-purpose flour

¹/₄ cup cornstarch

1 tablespoon baking powder

Freshly grated white pepper

2 cups cold dark beer

Olive or canola oil, for deep frying

1 Preheat the oven to 250°F. Line a platter with paper towels. Spread the eggplant slices on the paper towels and sprinkle them with the salt. Let them drain for 1¹/₂ hours, then blot them dry with fresh paper towels.

2 Line a 13 × 9-inch ovenproof dish with foil. Heat the oil in a large cast-iron or nonstick skillet. Add several eggplant slices at a time and cook until they begin to brown on each side, flipping once. When they are done, place them in the foil-lined dish place in the oven to keep warm.

3 Prepare the sauce: Place the roasted peppers, garlic, basil, lemon juice, mustard, and salt and pepper in a food processor. Blend well into a smooth puree.

4 Heat the heavy cream in a nonstick saucepan over medium-low heat. Add the pepper mixture gradually, stirring continually. The sauce should be thick and smooth.

5 When ready to serve, place two or three eggplant slices on each plate and top with the sauce. Serve hot.

Eggplant in Red Pepper Sauce

Makes 6 servings

3 large eggplants, sliced into ¹/₂-inch slices
1 tablespoon salt
Olive oil

Sauce:

4 sweet red peppers, roasted, seeded, peeled, and quartered
4 cloves garlic, roasted, peeled, and minced
¹/₃ cup fresh basil leaves
1 tablespoon lemon juice
1 teaspoon Dijon mustard
Salt and freshly ground pepper
1 cup heavy cream

Eggplant Puree

Makes 4–6 servings

6 tablespoons olive oil or butter

3 medium eggplants, cubed

3 medium onions, chopped coarsely

1½ cups milk

Salt and freshly ground pepper

½ tablespoon nutmeg

2 tablespoons butter

Freshly chopped chervil, to garnish

1 Place the oil, eggplant, and onion in a large nonstick saucepan. Sauté over medium-low heat until the eggplant is cooked to a golden brown.

2 Add the milk, salt and pepper, and nutmeg. Stir well and cover the pan. Continue to cook over medium-low heat, stirring occasionally. Cook for about 15–20 minutes, checking to see if more milk may be necessary, until the liquid is absorbed. Use a masher to puree, add the butter, and mix well.

3 Serve hot, sprinkled with chervil.

Belgian Endives in Béchamel Sauce

Makes 6 servings

6 medium endives, trimmed and left whole
1 large onion, chopped coarsely
Sea salt and white pepper
$1/2$ cup white dry wine
1 cup grated Emmentaler or Swiss cheese

Béchamel Sauce:
3 tablespoons butter or olive oil
3 teaspoons cornstarch or all-purpose flour
$1^1/2$ cups milk
Salt and freshly ground pepper
A pinch grated nutmeg

1 Preheat the oven to 350°F. Generously butter a large nonstick skillet. Add the endives and onion. Sauté over medium heat, turning the endives until they brown on all sides. Add a pinch of sea salt and pepper. Add the wine, cover the pot, lower heat to medium-low, and simmer for 25–30 minutes, until the liquid has evaporated. Remove the skillet from the heat.

2 Meanwhile, prepare the Béchamel Sauce: Melt the butter over medium-low heat in a nonstick saucepan. Dissolve the cornstarch in the milk and add gradually to the melted butter, stirring continually. Add a pinch each of salt, pepper, and nutmeg, continuing to stir until a thick consistency is reached.

3 Generously butter a 9 × 9-inch ovenproof dish. Pour in half of the béchamel and run it over the bottom of the whole dish. Arrange the endives and the onion, evenly, on the béchamel. Pour the remaining béchamel on the top of the vegetables. Sprinkle the grated cheese evenly over the whole top.

4 Bake for 30 minutes. The dish is done when the top turns brown and bubbly. Serve hot.

Cauliflower with Cherry Tomatoes

Makes 6–8 servings

1 large head cauliflower, trimmed and cut
    into small florets

1/2 cup extra-virgin olive oil

1 medium red onion, chopped

20 cherry tomatoes, cut into quarters
    and seeded

2 cloves garlic, minced

2 teaspoons lemon juice

1/3 cup fresh basil, chopped coarsely

1/3 cup flat-leaf Italian parsley, chopped finely

Sea salt and freshly ground pepper

1 Place the cauliflower in salted water to cover in a large saucepan. Bring to a boil and cook over medium heat for about 10 minutes, or until tender. Rinse and drain well under cold running water. Place in a large bowl and set aside.

2 Pour the olive oil into a large skillet, add the onion, tomatoes, and garlic, and cook over medium-low heat for 3–5 minutes, stirring often. Remove from the heat and add the lemon juice, basil, parsley, and salt and pepper to taste, and mix well.

3 Pour the tomato sauce over the cauliflower and toss gently.

NOTE: Serve warm or at room temperature as an accompaniment to a main course.

Parsnips and Carrots

Makes 8 servings

1 pound parsnips, washed well and sliced into
    disks (do not peel)
1 pound carrots, peeled and sliced into disks
4 cups water
Salt
1 teaspoon sugar
5 tablespoons butter or margarine,
    plus additional as needed
$1/4$ cup maple syrup
A pinch dry mustard
Finely chopped fresh parsley or chervil

1 Place the parsnips and carrots in a saucepan. Add the water and bring to a boil. Add salt and sugar. Lower the heat to medium-low. Cover and simmer gently for 20 minutes.

2 Just before serving, drain the vegetables. Melt the butter in the saucepan they were cooked in. Add the maple syrup and mustard. Mix well with a wooden spatula until a blended sauce forms. Add the vegetables and toss them gently until they are well coated with the sauce. Serve hot, sprinkled with parsley or chervil.

Leeks en Croûte in White Wine Sauce

Makes 6 servings

8 medium leeks, well washed, trimmed,
   and cut into 1-inch lenths
6 slices whole wheat bread
3 tablespoons butter
1 1/2 cups dry white wine
2 tablespoons cornstarch
Salt and freshly ground pepper
3 tablespoons heavy cream
Finely chopped fresh chives, for garnish

1 Preheat the oven to 250°F. Place the leeks in a large saucepan, add salted water to cover, and bring to a boil. Boil for about 10 minutes. Drain and set aside.

2 Trim the crusts from the bread slices. Melt about 1 tablespoon of butter in a large skillet and brown both sides of the slices lightly. Place in an ovenproof dish and keep warm in the oven.

3 Melt the remaining 2 tablespoons of butter in a large skillet. Add 1/2 cup of the white wine. Dissolve the cornstarch in the remaining 1 cup of wine and add to the skillet. Add salt and pepper and stir constantly until a roux is formed. Add the heavy cream and blend well. Add the leeks and toss gently with a wooden spoon. Allow the leeks to reheat.

4 Place one slice of warm bread on each serving plate. Place equal amounts of leek sauce on the top of the slices. Sprinkle with chives and serve hot.

Sweet Pea Mousse

Makes 6–8 servings

3 teaspoons butter

1 cup fresh or frozen sweet peas

1 medium-size onion, chopped finely

Salt and freshly ground white pepper

$^2/_3$ cup water

12 ounces cottage cheese

12 ounces ricotta cheese

$^1/_2$ cup fresh parsley, chopped finely

Mayonnaise:

1 egg yolk

1 teaspoon French, Dijon, or other
    prepared mustard

Salt and freshly ground white pepper

$^3/_4$ cup light olive oil

2 teaspoons vinegar, preferably tarragon
    vinegar

1 Melt the butter in a saucepan and add the peas, onion, and a pinch of salt. Stir well and sauté over medium-low heat, about 2 minutes.

2 Add the water, stir, and cover. Cook for 7–8 minutes, until all the liquid is absorbed. Remove from the heat

3 Prepare the Mayonnaise: Place the egg yolk in a deep bowl. Add the mustard, salt and pepper, and a few drops of the olive oil. Begin to mix with a whisk or a mixer (I always use a mixer). Keep adding the remaining oil little by little while continuing to mix. Toward the end, add the vinegar and continue to mix until a rich, thick consistency is reached. Keep the mayonnaise in the refrigerator until ready to be used.

4 In a large bowl, combine the cottage cheese, ricotta cheese, the pea mixture, and parsley, and mix well. Add 1 cup of Mayonnaise and blend thoroughly. Check the seasonings.

5 Choose a good mold for the mousse, hollow at the center. Cover the bottom part with plastic wrap for better unmolding. Pour the pea mixture into the mold and gently press it down with a spatula. Smooth the top level with the spatula. Place the mousse in the refrigerator for at least 2 hours before serving. Unmold it carefully onto a serving plate. Remove the plastic wrap and serve cold.

Glazed Onions and Shallots

Makes 8 servings

1 (10-ounce) package red pearl onions

1 (10-ounce) package golden pearl onions

10 ounces small (1-inch diameter) shallots

4 teaspoons butter

Salt and freshly ground pepper

1 cup ruby Port

1/3 cup low-salt vegetable stock

3 teaspoons red wine vinegar

1 Bring a large pot of salted water to a boil. Blanch the onions and shallots for 2 minutes. Drain. Peel the onions and shallots, trimming the ends.

2 Melt the butter in medium heavy skillet over medium-high heat. Add the onions and shallots. Stir to coat. Sprinkle with salt and pepper. Add the Port, stock, and vinegar, and bring to a simmer. Lower the heat to medium, cover, and simmer until the onions and shallots are tender, about 15 minutes. Uncover and simmer, stirring occasionally, until the liquid is reduced to a glaze, about 20 minutes. Season to taste with salt and pepper. Serve immediately or rewarm over low heat before serving.

Fava Bean and Potato Puree

Makes 4 servings

3 cups cooked fava beans

3 large potatoes, cooked and quartered

2 tablespoons plus 2 teaspoons butter

1 onion, chopped finely

A few fresh sage leaves, crumbled

Salt and freshly ground pepper

$\frac{1}{2}$ cup heavy cream

1 Place the fava beans and potatoes in a large saucepan and puree them with a masher until smooth.

2 Melt the 2 tablespoons butter in another saucepan and add the onion and sage. Sauté lightly over medium-low heat until the onions begin to soften. Sprinkle with salt and pepper and add the cream. Mix well.

3 Add the potato mixture and continue to stir until a rich, well-blended consistency is achieved. Add 2 teaspoons butter to the mixture and stir some more. Serve hot.

Stuffed **Tomatoes** Pyrenees **Style**

Makes 4 servings

1 Slice the tomatoes horizontally at the very top and save the tops. Carefully scoop out their insides with the help of a pointed spoon, then place upside down over a paper towel for about 15 minutes to drain them of their remaining juice.

2 Place in a deep bowl the eggs, onion, olives, capers, parsley, mayonnaise, lemon juice, and salt and pepper to taste. Mix well and keep refrigerated until ready to serve.

3 Place two lettuce leaves flat on each plate. Place a tomato on the top of each set of leaves. Fill each tomato to the very top with the egg mixture. Sprinkle with the reserved parsley and serve cold.

NOTE: This is an excellent summer appetizer.

4 large ripe tomatoes

4 hard-boiled eggs, peeled and chopped
   coarsely

1 small onion, minced finely

6 pitted black olives, chopped finely

3 tablespoons small capers

5 tablespoons finely chopped parsley
   (reserve some for garnish)

5 tablespoons Mayonnaise, prepared or
   homemade (page 220)

1 teaspoon lemon juice

Salt and freshly ground pepper

Lettuce leaves

1 Preheat the oven to 350°F. Cut the tops off of the tomatoes and save the tops. Carefully scoop out their insides with the help of a pointed spoon, then place upside down over a paper towel for about 15 minutes to drain them of their remaining juice. Reserve the insides for the sauce.

2 In a deep bowl, mash the goat cheese with a fork. Add the oil, basil, thyme, rosemary, garlic, salt and pepper, and bread crumbs. Mix well. Fill each tomato shell with the goat cheese mixture.

3 Generously butter a baking dish large enough to hold the tomatoes. Place the stuffed tomatoes upright in the dish. Bake for 25–30 minutes.

4 Make the sauce while the tomatoes bake: Pour the oil into a nonstick saucepan. Add the onion, the insides of the tomatoes, the basil, and salt and pepper, and cook over medium-low heat, stirring frequently, until a sauce forms. Make sure it does not dry out; if need be, add one or two more peeled, chopped tomatoes. When the sauce is done, turn off the heat and cover the saucepan.

5 When the tomatoes are baked, remove from the oven and place in individual serving dishes. Reheat the sauce briefly and pour it over the top of each tomato. Serve hot.

Riviera Stuffed Tomatoes

Makes 4–6 servings

6 medium ripe tomatoes

14 ounces goat cheese

8 tablespoons virgin olive oil

2 tablespoons fresh basil, finely snipped, or
    1 tablespoon dried

2 teaspoons fresh or 1 teaspoon dried thyme

2 teaspoons fresh or 1 teaspoon dried
    rosemary

1 clove garlic, minced finely

Salt and freshly ground pepper

8 teaspoons bread crumbs

Sauce:

3 tablespoons olive oil

1 onion, chopped finely

2 tablespoons fresh basil, finely snipped

Salt and freshly ground pepper

Zucchini
Ratatouille

Makes 6–8 servings

¹/₄ cup virgin olive oil

2 onions, chopped

6 tomatoes, peeled, seeded, and chopped
   coarsely

3 cloves garlic, minced

4 medium zucchini, sliced

1 bay leaf

¹/₂ teaspoon dried oregano

Salt and freshly ground pepper

1 Pour the oil into a large nonstick pot. Add the onion and sauté briefly over medium-low heat. Add the tomatoes and garlic. Stir. Cover the pot and cook for about 15 minutes.

2 Add the zucchini, bay leaf, oregano, and salt and pepper. Stir gently for a couple of minutes. Cover and continue to cook over medium-low heat, stirring occasionally, for another 20–30 minutes. Remove the bay leaf. Serve hot.

Easy Spinach Croquettes

Makes 8–10 servings

1 Boil the spinach in salted water for 3–4 minutes, or until well cooked. Drain thoroughly, squeezing out all the water.

2 Beat the eggs in a deep bowl. Add the milk and beat some more. Add the garlic, bread crumbs, cheese, salt and pepper, and spinach, and mix well. Place the bowl in the refrigerator for at least 2 hours, or until ready to serve.

3 Preheat the oven to 350°F. Generously butter one or two 8 × 8-inch oven-proof dishes. Moisten your hands with water and shape the spinach mixture into balls about 1¹/2 inches in diameter by rolling them carefully with both hands.

4 Carefully place the croquettes in the baking dish(es), leaving some space between the balls. Bake for 25–30 minutes. Serve warm.

1 pound fresh spinach, well washed and
   chopped finely

7 eggs

2 tablespoons milk

2 cloves garlic, minced finely

2 cups bread crumbs

1 cup grated Parmesan cheese

Salt and freshly ground pepper

Parsnip-Orange Puree

Makes 4–6 servings

14 large parsnips, scrubbed

$1/2$ heavy cream

$1/2$ cup orange juice

3 tablespoons butter

Salt and freshly ground pepper

$1/2$ teaspoon grated nutmeg

Finely chopped fresh parsley, for garnish

1 Preheat the oven to 250°F. Cut the parsnips into thin slices and place them in a large saucepan filled with water. Over medium heat bring the water to a boil, cover, and cook for about 30 minutes. Drain and allow to cool.

2 Puree the parsnips until smooth with a masher or by passing them through a sieve. Place back in the saucepan. Add the cream and orange juice. Cook over medium-low heat, stirring constantly, until most of the liquid is absorbed by the puree.

3 Add the butter, salt and pepper, and nutmeg. Blend well and serve hot, sprinkled with parsley. (If you prepare this ahead of time, generously butter an ovenproof dish, place the ungarnished puree in it, and keep warm in the oven until ready to serve). Just before serving, sprinkle with parsley.

Broccoli Rabe in Garlic

Makes 16 servings

³/₄ cup extra-virgin olive oil

12 large cloves garlic, sliced thinly and crushed

1 teaspoon dried crushed red pepper

4 pounds broccoli rabe (rapini), thick stems trimmed

Sea salt and freshly ground pepper

1 Heat the olive oil in a small saucepan over low heat. Add the garlic and simmer until very tender, about 3 minutes (do not brown). Remove from the heat and stir in the crushed red pepper.

2 Place the broccoli rabe in very large pot of boiling salted water and cook until tender, about 5 minutes. Drain well. Toss with the garlic and its oil. Season to taste with sea salt and pepper. Serve hot.

Potato, Leek, and Carrot Puree

Makes 6 servings

6 large potatoes, peeled and cubed

3 leeks, well washed, trimmed, and sliced,
  white and lower green parts only

3 long, thin carrots, peeled and sliced

5 tablespoons heavy cream

3 tablespoons butter

A pinch grated nutmeg

Salt and freshly ground pepper

1 Boil the vegetables in water to cover for 20–25 minutes. Add a pinch of salt toward the end of the boiling, if you wish, but use just a tiny bit. Drain, reserving 1/2 cup of the liquid (the rest can be saved as vegetable stock for soups or other uses).

2 Puree the vegetables in a food processor.

3 Pour the 1/2 cup of cooking liquid into an 11 × 7-inch casserole, add the pureed vegetables, and keep warm over low heat. Add the cream and mix well.

4 Melt the butter in a small skillet and stir into the puree. Add the nutmeg and salt and pepper. Blend well and serve as an accompaniment to the main course.

Mushrooms

oday, the trained cook knows that there are endless varieties of mushrooms to be found everywhere, making it possible to please and delight the most sophisticated palates. Mushrooms, or *funghi*, as they are called in Italy, were greatly appreciated in antiquity, especially in the ancient Mediterranean Roman world: Greece, France, Spain, Egypt, Italy, and so on. From there, their popularity spread to other parts of the world. Often, a certain aura of mystery surrounded their cultivation and the obscure places where they could be found. The ancients were very secretive about these places, which they considered almost sacred. Such was the high esteem they had for what they considered one of the healthiest and most delicious of foods. In Asia, especially in Japan and China, residents cultivated types different from those of the West, such as the shiitake, which was deeply appreciated for its taste as well as for what they considered its medicinal qualities. Even today, Asians attribute great healing powers to the consumption of mushrooms. This is one of the reasons why mushrooms occupy such an important role in Asian cuisine.

Moreover, nowadays, with increased travel and exchange between cuisines from other corners of the world, Americans have begun to discover the true charm of mushrooms and their ability to transform an everyday dish into a sublime one, brimming in wonderful textures and an "out of this world" flavor. In our times, we have become used to seeing mushrooms being used in the kitchen in multiple ways. They often accompany fish and meat dishes; they blend superbly with grains, pasta, and rice; they garnish beautifully certain salads, and they certainly supplement and transform a vegetarian plate into the food of paradise. All mushrooms, from the most ordinary white type we find often in supermarkets, *champignons de Paris* as they are called, to the most sophisticated chanterelles or truffles, surprise a cultivated palate by their intriguing textures and exquisite taste.

When preparing mushrooms for the table, we must give due attention to how they are cooked. Mushrooms have a very subtle and delicate nature, especially with regard to texture and flavor, and this must always be respected and, whenever possible, enhanced. Some mushrooms are enhanced by a few drops of lemon juice, white wine, spices, and herbs; some cooks go as far as marinating their mushrooms before they are cooked. All of this must be done with careful attention, using the enhancements in small quantities so as not to destroy the original flavors and texture of the mushrooms. Often, it is simpler to sauté them in butter over low or medium-low heat, in combination with either garlic, shallots, or onions, adding at the last minute a few drops of white wine, a pinch of sea salt and white pepper, and a little finely chopped fresh parsley; one ends up with a sublime mixture that is a fine accompaniment to a meat, fish, egg, or vegetable dish. All the mushroom recipes presented here are easy to prepare. I hope they give an incentive to the cook to keep experimenting with the rich and wide of varieties of mushrooms we find all around us. The exquisite simplicity of mushrooms makes them so charming, so appropriate, so straightforward for all kinds of creative and inventive of culinary uses.

Wild mushrooms are one of the last foraged, wild foods available to most cooks. Almost all of the other plants we use have long been domesticated and bred to emphasize qualities we find desirable. Wild mushrooms, on the other hand—with their woodsy, earthy, complex flavors and aromas, and their rich, primeval colors and forms—bring into our kitchens a reminder that all the places we inhabit were once wilderness.

—Alice Waters, *Chez Panisse Vegetables*

Mushroom Ragout

2 pounds fresh white mushrooms
   (*champignons de Paris*) cleaned and
   halved down the center
2 large portobello mushrooms, cleaned, sliced
   into 1¹/₂-inch cubes
12 shallots, peeled and quartered
8 tablespoons unsalted butter
3 tablespoons Cognac
1 cup white dry wine
1 bay leaf
²/₃ cup heavy cream
2 tablespoons good-quality paprika
Salt and freshly ground pepper
²/₃ cup fresh flat-leaf Italian parsley,
   chopped finely
1 cup sour cream

1 Place mushrooms, the shallots, and butter in a large, deep skillet. Cook gently over medium-low heat, stirring often, until the mixture begins to soften. Add the Cognac and continue to cook, stirring, for a minute or two. Add the white wine, bay leaf, heavy cream, paprika, and salt and pepper to taste. Stir gently.

2 Lower the heat to low, cover, and cook for 15–18 minutes. Remove the bay leaf. Set aside until ready to serve.

3 Just before serving, reheat the ragout over medium-low heat, adding the parsley and sour cream, stirring well. Serve hot as accompaniment to the main course.

Herb and Almond-Stuffed Mushrooms

1 Preheat the oven to 350°F.

2 Remove and chop the mushroom stems finely and place in a bowl. Add the oil, lemon juice, and salt and pepper. Mix well and set aside.

3 In a separate bowl, combine the milk, oil, and egg. Add the garlic, bread crumbs, almonds, all the herbs, and the lemon zest. Mix well. Add the mushroom mixture, check the seasonings, and mix thoroughly.

4 Spoon the mixture into the mushroom caps. Generously butter an 8 × 8-inch ovenproof dish and arrange the mushrooms in the dish, stuffed side up. Bake for 20–25 minutes. Remove from the oven, allow to cool for a few minutes, then serve at room temperature.

NOTE: The stuffed mushrooms can be served separately as hors d'oeuvres, or as an appetizer at the table. In this latter case, serve three mushrooms per person.

Makes 4 servings

12 large mushrooms, cleaned

12 tablespoons olive oil

1 tablespoon lemon juice

Salt and freshly ground pepper

$1/2$ cup milk

6 tablespoons olive oil

1 egg, beaten

2 cloves garlic, minced

$2/3$ cup bread crumbs

$1/4$ cup almonds, chopped

1 tablespoon dried or 3 tablespoons fresh rosemary

1 tablespoon dried 3 tablespoons fresh thyme

1/3 cup fresh parsley, minced

1 tablespoon dried or 3 tablespoons fresh chives

Zest of 1 small lemon, minced finely

Porcini
Mushrooms
au Gratin

Makes 4–6 servings

2 tablespoons butter

4 shallots, chopped finely

1 pound fresh porcini mushrooms, cleaned
   and trimmed

Salt

1 tablespoon lemon juice

$\frac{1}{2}$ cup heavy cream

3 tablespoons Calvados liqueur

Grated Parmesan cheese

1 Preheat the oven to 300°F.

2 Melt the butter in a large nonstick skillet. Add the shallots and sauté gently over medium-low heat.

3 Remove the stems from the mushrooms and chop coarsely. Slice the mushroom caps in half.

4 Add the salt, lemon juice, mushroom caps, and stems to the shallots, cover, and, stirring occasionally, continue to cook over medium-low heat for 8–10 minutes.

5 Add the heavy cream and Calvados. Stir well and continue to cook for another 3–5 minutes.

6 Generously butter an 8 × 8-inch ovenproof dish. Place the mushroom mixture in it, distributing the mixture evenly in the dish. Sprinkle with the cheese and bake for about 15 minutes. Serve hot.

Mushrooms en Croûte

1 Preheat the oven to 250°F. Trim the crusts from the bread.

2 Melt 1 tablespoon of the butter in a large skillet, brown the bread slices on both sides, then place them on an ovenproof plate and keep warm in the oven.

3 Melt the remaining 2 tablespoons of butter in a large skillet. Add the shallots, mushrooms, salt and pepper, and wine, and sauté over medium-low heat, stirring often, until the mushrooms are cooked. Add the cream and continue to stir until a well-blended sauce is achieved.

4 Place one slice of bread on each serving plate. Divide the mushroom sauce among the slices and serve hot. Garnish with chervil or parsley if using.

NOTE: This is an excellent appetizer.

4 slices whole wheat bread

3 tablespoons butter

5 shallots, chopped

16 mushrooms, cleaned, stems trimmed, caps sliced

Salt and freshly ground pepper

3 tablespoons white dry wine

$1/2$ cup heavy cream

Finely chopped fresh chervil or parsley, for garnish (optional)

Spinach with Portobello Mushrooms

Makes 6 servings

1 pound fresh spinach, well washed
    and trimmed
10 tablespoons extra-virgin olive oil, plus
    extra if needed
8 portobello mushrooms, cleaned, trimmed,
    and sliced
1 large Vidalia or Spanish onion, sliced
Salt and freshly ground pepper
A pinch grated nutmeg

1 Place the spinach plus water to cover in a saucepan. Bring to a boil, lower the heat to medium, cover, and simmer gently for about 30 minutes. Drain thoroughly.

2 While the spinach is cooking, place the oil, mushrooms, and onion in a large nonstick skillet. Sauté over medium-low heat for 8–10 minutes, stirring frequently, until the onion turns golden. Add more oil if necessary.

3 Add the spinach, salt and pepper, and nutmeg. Stir frequently until well blended. Check the seasonings and serve hot.

NOTE: This is an excellent accompaniment to a fish, meat, or egg main course.

Potato and Mushroom Stew

Makes 6–8 servings

1 Cook the potatoes in boiling salted water for about 3 minutes. Drain completely and set aside.

2 Pour the oil into a nonstick casserole, raise the heat to medium-high, add the mushrooms and onion, and sauté for 2 minutes. Lower the heat to low and add $1/2$ cup of the wine. Cover the casserole and simmer for 15 minutes.

3 Dissolve the cornstarch in the remaining $1/2$ cup of the wine and add to the stew. Add the bay leaves, the drained potatoes, a pinch of salt and pepper, and stir well. Cover and continue to simmer for another 15–20 minutes, until the vegetables are tender and the mixture has turned into a stew. (Add more wine if necessary.) Stir well, remove the bay leaves.

NOTE: Serve as an accompaniment to a fish, egg, or meat main course.

1 pound Idaho potatoes, peeled and cut into
    1-inch cubes
8 tablespoons olive oil
1 pound mushrooms, trimmed and halved
1 large onion, chopped
1 cup dry white wine
$1/2$ teaspoon cornstarch
2 bay leaves
Salt and freshly ground pepper

Mushrooms à la Bordelaise

Makes 4–6 servings

2 pounds mushrooms, cleaned and trimmed, caps and stems separated

4 tablespoons lemon juice

Salt

$\frac{1}{2}$ cup olive oil

$\frac{1}{2}$ cup dry white Bordeaux wine

4 shallots, minced

3 cloves garlic, minced

Freshly ground pepper

Finely chopped fresh parsley, for garnish

1 Place the mushroom caps in a big bowl and add the lemon juice and a pinch of salt. Mix well and let stand. Place the stems aside.

2 Pour $\frac{1}{4}$ cup of the olive oil into a large non-stick skillet and heat over medium-high heat. When the oil is hot, add the the mushroom caps and sauté for about 2 minutes per side, turning them once. Lower the heat to low and add the wine. Cover and simmer gently, stirring occasionally, for about 30 minutes.

3 Finely chop the mushroom stems and place them in a separate skillet. Add the remaining $\frac{1}{4}$ cup oil, shallots, garlic, and a pinch of salt and pepper, and sauté over medium-low heat for about 2 minutes, stirring frequently.

4 Just before serving, add the shallot mixture to the rest of the mushrooms and mix well. Check the seasonings and serve hot, sprinkled with parsley.

NOTE: This is an excellent accompaniment to any main course.

Saint Seraphim's
Mushroom
Sauce

Makes 1¹/4 cups

1 ounce butter or margarine

3 shallots, chopped finely

¹/2 pound mushrooms, sliced

1 cup sherry or white wine

¹/2 teaspoon ground turmeric

¹/2 cup fresh parsley, chopped finely

Salt and freshly ground pepper

Melt the butter in an enameled or stainless-steel saucepan. Add the shallots, mushrooms, wine, turmeric, and salt and pepper, and cook for a few minutes, until the mushrooms begin to brown. Lower the heat and add the parsley, stirring continually. Cook for another 4–5 minutes, until the sauce is done.

NOTE: This sauce is excellent on top of rice, fish, meat and eggs.

Portobellos in Port Wine Sauce

Makes 4–6 servings

Juice of 1 lemon

1¹/₂ pounds portobello mushrooms, cleaned, stems removed (use them for another purpose)

2 ounces butter

Salt

1 cup red Port wine

5 tablespoons heavy cream

1 egg yolk, beaten

Freshly ground pepper

1 Preheat the oven to 350°F. Pour the lemon juice into a bowl filled with cold water. Add the mushrooms and let stand for 30 minutes. Drain thoroughly and slice in half.

2 Melt the butter in a large nonstick skillet over medium heat. Add the mushrooms and a pinch of salt, and sauté them for 10–12 minutes, stirring frequently.

3 Mix the Port and heavy cream in a saucepan. Stirring, bring to a rapid boil. Remove from the heat, allow to cool a bit, and whisk in the egg yolk. Add salt and pepper and stir well.

5 Generously butter a 9 × 9-inch ovenproof dish. Spread the mushrooms evenly in the dish. Pour the sauce over the mushrooms. Bake for 10–15 minutes.

NOTE: Serve hot, as a side dish to the main course, or as an appetizer at an elegant dinner.

Mushrooms à la Barigoule

Makes 4–6 servings

6 tablespoons extra-virgin olive oil

1 onion, chopped

2 carrots, peeled and cut into small cubes

1 pound mushrooms, cleaned, trimmed, and
    halved lengthwise

Salt and freshly ground pepper

1 cup white dry wine

3 cloves garlic, minced

5 tablespoons water

Finely chopped fresh parsley, for garnish

1 Pour the oil into a cast-iron or nonstick casserole and add the onion and carrots. Place the mushrooms on top and sprinkle with salt and pepper. Cover and cook over medium-low heat for 3–4 minutes.

2 Add the wine, garlic, and water. Stir well, cover, and lower the heat to low. Continue to cook for 15 minutes. Remove the lid and continue to cook for another 5 minutes, until the liquid has reduced to one-third or less of its original amount. Check the seasonings, sprinkle with parsley.

NOTE: Serve as an accompaniment to the main course.

Part Four

Meal Accents

Salads, Sauces, and Breads

Salads

oday salads are deeply appreciated by all, no matter where they appear in the meal. They can be the perfect starter, an attractive main course, or a charming in-between or even culmination to an appetizing meal. During the summer months, I often put a great emphasis on the salad as a main course at least several times each week. Besides helping to simplify the task of food preparation during the hot-weather months, salad is a natural answer to a monastic diet that stresses the consumption of vegetables, grains, fruits, and low-fat foods.

Salads, like soups, have always played an integral role in the cooking of our monastery. Monastic cooking is well known for its simplicity, wholesomeness, sobriety, and good taste.

These basic principles mark a certain approach to cooking and are reflected in the dishes presented here. Both salads and soups are seen as perfect prototypes for these principles and, as such, are considered quintessentially monastic types of food.

These salad recipes have been tested again and again in our kitchen and served to the many guests who frequent our small guesthouse during the year. All our visitors have found them not only satisfactory but, as one of them whispered in my ear, "worthy of sharing with the wider public at large." Still, these recipes remain, as they should, faithful to their monastic/vegetarian inspiration. They exalt the values of health, freshness, nutrition, and basic good taste. A good salad, when carefully prepared and assembled, is always an occasion for celebration.

The salad we were dreaming of was another thing altogether: a salad of small, wild-tasting leaves like the mesclun in salads in the south of France. *Mesclun* is a Provencal word that means "mixed." Traditionally, mesclun was picked wild—a mixture of the shoots and leaves of the tender edible plants that start poking up on the hillsides after the rain in winter and early spring.

—Alice Waters, *Chez Panisse Vegetables*

Goat Cheese Salad Alpine Style

Makes 4–6 servings

½ loaf fresh French bread—a good healthy
    baguette, if possible—sliced into
    large cubes

2 cloves garlic, chopped into small pieces

10 tablespoons extra-virgin olive oil

1 pound cherry tomatoes

1 small red onion, chopped finely

6 ounces French goat cheese, cut carefully
    into cubes or bite-size pieces

12 fresh basil leaves, chopped coarsely

Vinaigrette:

3 tablespoons extra-virgin olive oil

2 tablespoons white wine vinegar

Sea salt and freshly ground pepper

1 Place the bread cubes into a large skillet. Add the garlic and the olive oil. Sauté over medium-low heat, stirring continually, for 5 minutes or so, until the bread browns slightly. Transfer a large salad bowl and let cool for a few minutes.

2 Add the tomatoes and onion and toss gently. Add the cheese and basil and toss once more.

3 Prepare the vinaigrette: mix all ingredients well in a small bowl and, just before serving, pour over the salad. Toss gently until all the salad ingredients are evenly coated. Serve at room temperature.

Lentil and Celery Heart Salad

1 Bring water to a boil in a large saucepan. Add the carrots and lentils. Cook over medium heat for 40–45 minutes. Rinse and drain under cold water. Allow to cool.

2 Transfer the carrots and lentils to a large salad bowl. Add the celery heart, onion, and cucumber. Toss gently and mix well. Place the bowl in the refrigerator until ready to serve.

3 Before serving, prepare the vinaigrette: mix all ingredients well in a small bowl. Pour the vinaigrette over the salad and toss gently, making sure all the salad ingredients are evenly coated. Serve the salad cold, sprinkled with parsley.

Makes 4–6 servings

2 medium carrots, peeled and cubed

$1/2$ cup dried lentils, preferably French Le Puy

1 celery heart, sliced thinly

1 small red onion, chopped finely

1 medium cucumber, peeled, seeded, and diced

Finely chopped fresh parsley, for garnish

Vinaigrette:

8 tablespoons extra-virgin olive oil

4 teaspoons freshly squeezed lemon juice

Salt and freshly ground pepper

Panzanella

Makes 6–8 servings

6 cups cubed stale country-style bread

10 medium ripe tomatoes, seeded
    and cubed

1 red onion, chopped finely

1 medium cucumber, peeled, seeded, and diced

8 pitted black olives, chopped

6 pitted green olives, chopped

$\frac{1}{2}$ cup fresh basil leaves, cut into thin strips

1 tablespoon fresh or $\frac{1}{2}$ tablespoon
    dried thyme

Vinaigrette:

8 tablespoons extra-virgin olive oil

4 tablespoons red wine vinegar

Salt and freshly ground pepper

1 Place the bread, tomatoes, onion, cucumber, and olives in a large salad bowl. Add the basil and thyme and toss.

2 Prepare the vinaigrette: Mix all ingredients well in a small bowl. Pour the vinaigrette slowly over the salad and toss gently. Set the salad aside (not in the refrigerator) for about 30 minutes, until the bread cubes soften. Just before serving, check the seasonings and adjust accordingly.

NOTE: This salad is always served at room temperature.

Zucchini
Salad Basque Style

1 Place the zucchini cubes in a large saucepan, add water to cover, and bring to a rapid boil, 3 minutes, maximum. Drain and rinse under cold running water.

2 Place the tomatoes, pepper, and onion in a salad bowl. Add the zucchini.

3 Prepare the vinaigrette: Mix all ingredients well in a small bowl. Just before serving, pour the vinaigrette over the vegetables and toss gently until they are evenly coated. Sprinkle with parsley and serve immediately.

Makes 6–8 servings

3 medium zucchini, cubed

4 medium ripe tomatoes, peeled, seeded, and chopped

1 sweet red pepper, seeded and cubed

1 medium red onion, chopped coarsely

Finely chopped fresh parsley, for garnish

Vinaigrette:

8 tablespoons extra-virgin olive oil

3 tablespoons wine vinegar

Salt and freshly ground pepper

Frisée Greens, Watercress, and Orange Salad

1 Peel the oranges, removing the white pith. Separate into segments and place in a salad bowl. Separate the frisée into individual leaves and add to the bowl. Add the watercress and onion, and mix well.

2 Prepare the vinaigrette: Mix all ingredients well in a small bowl. Let stand for at least 30 minutes at room temperature before stirring once again and pouring onto the salad. Just before ready to serve, add the dressing to the salad bowl and toss gently. Serve the salad in individual salad plates.

NOTE: This is a light, refreshing salad to serve after a heavy course.

Makes 6–8 servings

3 medium oranges

1 medium head of fresh frisée (curly endive), washed and trimmed

1 bunch of watercress, washed, stems trimmed

1 medium-size red onion, cut into thin slices

Vinaigrette:

8 tablespoons extra-virgin olive oil

3 tablespoons wine vinegar

1 tablespoon honey

1 teaspoon Dijon mustard

1 teaspoon grated orange peel

Salt and freshly ground pepper

Early Spring Salad

Makes 4–6 servings

1 large bunch fresh radishes, trimmed and
     quartered lengthwise
1 (12-ounce) goat cheese roll, cut into slices
1 small bunch fresh chives, chopped finely
A few sprigs chervil, chopped finely

Vinaigrette:
6 tablespoons extra-virgin olive oil
3 teaspoons white wine vinegar
Salt and freshly ground pepper

1 Place the radishes in a salad bowl and add
the cheese. (Alternatively, the cheese slices can
be put under the broiler for a few seconds
before placing with the radishes; let them melt
a bit, as they do in France, before serving. In
that case the salad should be served warm.)
Add the chives and chervil.

2 Prepare the vinaigrette: Mix all ingredients
well in a small bowl. Just before serving, pour
the dressing over the salad and toss gently.
Serve immediately.

NOTE: This salad can be a perfect appetizer
during the early spring months, when the first
radishes, chives, and chervil begin to appear in
our gardens.

Beet, Tangerine, and Arugula
Salad

Makes 6 servings

1 pound beets (about 5 medium), well
    washed and trimmed
5 tangerines, peeled, seeded, and separated
1 medium red onion, chopped coarsely
1 bunch of fresh arugula

Vinaigrette:

6 tablespoons extra-virgin olive oil
3 tablespoons white wine vinegar
1 tablespoon Dijon mustard
Salt and freshly ground pepper

1 Cook the beets in boiling salted water for 18–20 minutes, until tender. Drain, let cool, then peel. Cut the beets in half, then slice them evenly. Place in a bowl. Add the tangerines and the onions.

2 Divide the arugula greens equally among six serving plates.

3 Prepare the vinaigrette: Whisk all ingredients well in a small bowl until smooth. Pour over the beet mixture and toss gently. Divide this mixture equally among the plates, atop the greens. Serve immediately.

Provençale Mesclun Salad with Goat Cheese

1 Place the mesclun in a salad bowl. Add the onion and toss gently.

2 Preheat the oven to 350°F or preheat the broiler. Place the bread slices in a single layer in an ovenproof dish. Place one slice of goat cheese (or crumble it) on top of each bread slice. Sprinkle the olive oil on the cheese and top with a rosemary sprig, pressing it down into the cheese. Heat either in the oven or under the broiler until the cheese bubbles and begins to melt.

3 Prepare the vinaigrette: Mix all ingredients well in a small bowl. Pour the dressing over the salad, toss, and then distribute it equally among six serving plates.

4 Place one cheese-topped bread slice in the center of each salad plate. Serve immediately.

Makes 4–6 servings

1 pound mesclun (tender mixed salad greens), washed and dried

1 small red onion, sliced thinly

Extra-virgin olive oil

6 slices French bread

6 slices goat cheese

6 sprigs rosemary or thyme

Vinaigrette:

8 tablespoons olive oil

3 tablespoons wine vinegar

1 teaspoon lemon juice

Salt and freshly ground pepper

Jerusalem Artichoke
Salad

Makes 6 servings

30 Jerusalem artichokes

3 cups dry white wine

1 cup walnuts

1 medium red onion, sliced thinly

7 tablespoons extra-virgin olive oil

3 tablespoons lemon juice

Salt and freshly ground pepper

$1/3$ cup finely chopped chervil or parsley,
    for garnish

Vinaigrette:

6 tablespoons extra-virgin olive oil

3 teaspoons white wine vinegar

Salt and freshly ground pepper

1 Clean the Jerusalem artichokes thoroughly (and, if you wish, peel them). Place in a large casserole dish, add the wine, and bring to a boil. Lower the heat to medium and cook for 12–15 minutes. Drain and allow to cool. Cut each Jerusalem artichoke into quarters or slice, and transfer to a salad bowl.

2 Place the walnuts in a saucepan, add water to cover, and bring to a boil. Boil for 5 minutes. Drain and then crumble the walnuts with a knife. Add the walnuts and the sliced onion to the salad bowl.

3 Prepare the vinaigrette: Mix all ingredients well in a small bowl. Pour over the salad and toss gently, until the salad ingredients are evenly coated. Distribute the salad in equal portions among six serving plates, and sprinkle with chopped chervil or parsley.

NOTE: This is an excellent appetizer any time of the year.

Apple, Endive, and Celery Root Salad

1 Combine the apples, endive, and raisins in a large bowl.

2 Just before serving, prepare the vinaigrette: Combine all ingredients in a small bowl. Mix well. Pour it over the apple mixture and toss to coat.

3 Place the shredded celery root in a separate bowl and add the mayonnaise, lemon juice, and salt and pepper. Mix well. Chill the two salad bowls in the refrigerator for 1–2 hours before serving.

4 When ready to serve, place one or two (depending on size) lettuce leaves in the center of each serving plate. Place on half of the lettuce leaf a mound of the apple mixture, and on the other half a mound of the celery root salad. Serve immediately, for the salad must be served cold.

Makes 4–6 servings

4 ripe Golden Delicious apples, peeled, cored, and cut into thin slices

1 Belgian endive, sliced thinly

4 tablespoons raisins

2$\frac{1}{2}$ cups shredded celery root

3 tablespoons low-fat mayonnaise

2 tablespoons lemon juice

Salt and freshly ground pepper

Lettuce leaves, for serving

Vinaigrette:

1 tablespoon sugar

7 tablespoons sesame oil or vegetable oil

3 tablespoons cider vinegar

Salt and freshly ground pepper

Grated Carrot and Black Olive Salad

Makes 6–8 servings

10 large carrots, peeled and julienned

6 sprigs parsley, chopped finely

3 shallots, sliced thinly

30 medium pitted black olives

Dressing:

8 tablespoons extra-virgin olive oil

4 tablespoons wine vinegar

1 1/2 tablespoons Dijon mustard

Salt and freshly ground pepper

1 Place the carrots in a large, deep bowl. Add the parsley, shallots, and olives. Mix well.

2 Prepare the dressing: In a separate bowl, combine all ingredients. Mix thoroughly with a fork until smooth.

3 Pour the dressing over the carrot mixture and mix well. Refrigerate the salad and keep cold until ready to serve.

NOTE: This is an interesting and easy-to-make appetizer to serve during the warm days of the summer.

Asparagus and Artichokes in Tarragon Vinaigrette

Makes 6 servings

24 fresh asparagus spears, trimmed

36 fresh spinach leaves, well washed and trimmed

1 (16-ounce) jar or can artichoke hearts in brine, drained

2 hard-boiled eggs, peeled and crumbled finely

3 teaspoons finely chopped fresh tarragon, for garnish

Vinaigrette:

8 tablespoons extra-virgin olive oil

3 tablespoons heavy cream

1 teaspoon French mustard

4 tablespoons tarragon-scented vinegar

Salt and freshly ground pepper

1 Cook the asparagus in boiling salted water for 3–4 minutes. Rinse under cold running water. Drain thoroughly and dry with paper towels. Set aside.

3 Prepare the vinaigrette: Mix the oil, cream, and mustard in a medium-size bowl. Whisk the mixture with a mixer. Add the vinegar and salt and pepper, and continue whisking until the vinaigrette achieves a smooth and creamy consistency.

4 Place six spinach leaves in a decorative form on each of six serving plates. Arrange four asparagus spears on one side and two artichoke hearts on the other. Pour some of the vinaigrette over vegetables, starting at the center. Garnish with crumbled egg, then sprinkle with tarragon. Serve at room temperature.

Spanish Spinach Salad

Makes 6–8 servings

1 pound fresh spinach, well washed
    and trimmed

22 asparagus spears

1/2 cup grated cheddar cheese

3 hard-boiled eggs, peeled and crumbled

4 tablespoons pignoli (pine nuts)

1 small red onion, sliced thinly into circles

Dressing:

6 tablespoons extra-virgin olive oil

3 tablespoons lemon juice

2 tablespoons French mustard

4 teaspoons mayonnaise (commercial is fine)

1 teaspoon dried or 3 teaspoons fresh tarragon,
    chopped if fresh

Salt and freshly ground pepper

1 Place the spinach in a large salad bowl.

2 Boil the asparagus in salted water for 5 minutes. Drain and slice into 2-inch lengths. Add to the spinach, along with the cheese, eggs, pignoli, and onion. Mix gently by hand.

3 Just before serving, prepare the dressing: Place all ingredients in a small bowl and whisk them by hand. Pour the dressing over the salad and toss gently. Serve immediately.

Potato, Leek, and Egg Salad

1 Peel the potatoes and place them in a large saucepan filled with water. Heat the pan over medium heat. Boil the potatoes for about 15 minutes, until they are tender. Drain.

3 Meanwhile, boil the leeks separately in salted water for about 15 minutes, until they are cooked. Drain.

4 Prepare the vinaigrette: Mix all ingredients well in a small bowl.

5 Place some of the potatoes and two egg halves on the center of each of 6 plates and gently curve the leeks in a circle around them. Pour the vinaigrette equally over each serving, and sprinkle with scallions. Serve at room temperature.

Makes 6 servings

1 pound small potatoes (preferably new and tender)

6 leeks, white parts only, well washed and trimmed

6 hard-boiled eggs, peeled and sliced in half lengthwise

1 bunch scallions, thinly sliced, for garnish

Vinaigrette:

6 tablespoons extra-virgin olive oil

3 tablespoons tarragon scented vinegar

$1/2$ teaspoon French mustard

Salt and freshly ground pepper

Bethlehem Salad

1 In a small skillet, combine the walnuts, butter, and salt and pepper to taste. Stir over medium-low heat until the walnuts turn golden, 2 or 3 minutes. Set aside.

2 Separate the curly frisée into individual leaves and place in a deep salad bowl.

3 Cut the Belgian endives crosswise into thin slices and add them to the bowl. Add the onion and mix well. Add the olive oil, lemon juice, and salt and pepper to taste. Add the cooked walnuts. Toss gently and serve at room temperature.

NOTE: This is a perfect salad to serve between the main course and the dessert.

Makes 4–6 servings

$1/2$ cup chopped walnuts

1 tablespoon butter

Salt and freshly ground pepper

1 medium head of frisée (curly endive) well washed and dried

2 small Belgian endives

1 small red onion, cut into thin half-moons

4 tablespoons extra-virgin olive oil

2 teaspoons fresh lemon juice

Sauces

In France, where the art of sauce preparation has been perfected throughout the centuries, chefs as well as ordinary cooks have used the sauce as a way of enhancing the taste and presentation of a particular dish. These chefs have also provided us with boundless varieties of sauces and relishes to complement almost any culinary concoction. Some of the recipes presented here are traditional ones, and others represent some of the newer, lighter, trends in sauce making. In either case, be it traditional or one of the more innovative types, they all serve the same purpose: that of enhancing and elevating what could be considered a simple ordinary plate to one of superb and superior quality. Vegetables are particularly delicious when they are served with a well-prepared sauce. They complement each other perfectly! Take for instance asparagus served with the traditional hollandaise, or hard-boiled eggs served with a homemade mayonnaise, or artichokes or beets served with

aioli sauce. As I said before, when it comes to sauces, the varieties are endless. The same can be said of the immense possibilities of vinaigrette dressing available today for any type of salad. The recipes presented here are but just a few suggestions.

Recently, I had the chance to visit with a good chef from France staying with us for a few days. Since he is reputed for the good sauces he invents and prepares in his restaurant in France, I asked him his secret. He replied simply by saying, "To present a good plate at the table you need to start with excellent ingredients." He continued, "To obtain an appetizing and tasty sauce, you must have available natural aromatic stock or juices, good-quality wine, and in certain cases fine liqueurs just right for the occasion. And at the end, while you try to obtain a sauce of superb quality, be always mindful not to try too hard and go too far and thus fall into excess. Your aim must always be the perfect balance, the right blending of all ingredients."

I like fresh mayonnaise so much I often smear it on bread for a snack. The bread, of course is merely a vehicle for the lemony yellow sauce. Use it as a basic summer recipe; it goes well with any blanched summer vegetable or on any sandwich, for that matter, with or without vegetables. Mayonnaise is also lovely with herbs swirled into it.

—Amanda Hesser, *The Cook & The Gardener*

Béchamel Sauce

Makes about 2 cups

2 tablespoons butter or margarine

2 tablespoons cornstarch or flour

1¹/₂ cups milk

3 tablespoons dry vermouth (optional)

Salt and freshly ground pepper

A pinch grated nutmeg

Melt the butter in a medium stainless-steel pan over medium-low heat. Add the cornstarch, stirring continually with a whisk. Add the milk little by little while whisking continually. Add the vermouth, salt and pepper, and nutmeg, and continue to stir. When the sauce begins to boil, lower the heat and continue cooking until it thickens.

NOTE: This sauce is excellent with fish and vegetables, and it is a necessary base for soufflés, omelets, and other egg dishes.

Mornay Sauce

Makes 2 cups

1¹/₂ cups Béchamel Sauce

4 tablespoons grated Gruyère cheese

4 tablespoons Romano or Parmesan cheese

10 tablespoons heavy cream

Heat the Béchamel Sauce in a medium stainless-steel pan over medium-low heat. When the sauce is at the boiling point, add the cheese and let it melt as the sauce thickens. When the sauce is ready, remove it from the heat and add the heavy cream while stirring continually with a whisk or mixer.

Monastery
Mushroom Sauce

Makes about 2 cups

2 cups mushrooms, trimmed and sliced

4 tablespoons butter

4 shallots, or 1 medium onion, diced

2 cloves garlic, minced

6 tablespoons dry white wine

1 cup heavy cream

Salt and freshly ground pepper

Finely chopped fresh chervil

1 Boil the mushrooms in salted water for 12–15 minutes. Drain and puree in a food processor. Set aside.

2 Melt the butter in a nonstick saucepan and add the shallots and garlic. Sauté over low heat for 2 or 3 minutes, stirring constantly.

3 Add the wine and mix well. Add the cream and stir. Add the pureed mushrooms, salt and pepper to taste, and some chervil. Continue to stir until well blended.

NOTE: This delicious sauce goes well with egg noodles, pasta, rice, fish, certain vegetables, and egg dishes.

White Sauce

In a small bowl, dissolve the cornstarch into $1/2$ cup of the milk. Melt the butter in a medium stainless-steel pan over medium heat. When the butter begins to foam, add the cornstarch mixture, stirring continuously. Add the rest of the milk and the salt, pepper, and nutmeg, and continue to cook, stirring, until the sauce comes to a boil. Lower the heat and continue to cook, stirring, until the sauce thickens. The sauce is ready when it is smooth and thick.

NOTE: This sauce can be used as a basis for many other useful variations, and can also be used by itself on fish, meats, eggs, and vegetables.

Makes $1^{1}/2$ cups

2 tablespoons cornstarch or flour
$1^{1}/2$ cups milk
2 tablespoons butter or margarine
Salt and freshly ground black pepper
A pinch of grated nutmeg

White Sauce with Wine

Makes $1^{3}/4$ cups

Prepare the White Sauce as directed but do not add the nutmeg. Add $1/4$ cup of white wine or vermouth and $1/2$ teaspoon of dry mustard. Mix thoroughly.

White Sauce with Mustard

Makes $1^{1}/2$ cups

Prepare the White Sauce as directed. Add 2 teaspoons of French mustard and mix thoroughly.

Sauce Provençale

1 Pour the oil into a nonstick casserole and heat over medium heat. Add the tomatoes, onion, carrot, garlic, olives, bay leaf, thyme, and salt and pepper. Cook for about 5 minutes, then lower the heat to medium-low. Stir well.

2 Cover the casserole and gently simmer the sauce, stirring from time to time. If the heat seems high, lower it to low. Cook for 25–30 minutes. Check the seasonings and serve.

NOTE: This sauce is excellent with pasta, polenta, rice, certain fish, and vegetables.

Makes about 2 cups

6 tablespoons virgin olive oil

1 pound ripe tomatoes, peeled, seeded, and quartered

1 large onion, chopped coarsely

1 medium carrot, peeled and sliced thinly

3 cloves garlic, minced

1 (10-ounce) can pitted black olives, drained

1 bay leaf

A pinch fresh or dried thyme

Salt and freshly ground pepper

Pesto Sauce

Makes 1 cup

6 cloves garlic, minced

$1/2$ cup finely chopped fresh basil leaves

$1/2$ cup well-chopped shelled pistachio nuts

1 cup olive oil

8 teaspoons grated Parmesan cheese

A pinch salt

Place the garlic and basil in a mortar and mash with a pestle. Add the pistachio nuts and continue to mash thoroughly. Place the mixture in a larger container, add the olive oil gradually, then the cheese and salt, and blend thoroughly. Alternatively, a simpler and quicker way to prepare the pesto sauce is to place all the ingredients in a blender and mix thoroughly.

NOTE: This is usually served with pasta but it can also be used with gnocchi, seafood, eggs, and certain vegetables, such as zucchini.

Red Wine
Sauce

Makes 2 cups

3 shallots, chopped finely

5 tablespoons water

2 cups good red wine, such as Bordeaux

1 bay leaf

4 tablespoons butter

A pinch cayenne

Salt and freshly ground pepper

4 tablespoons water

1 teaspoon cornstarch

1 Place the shallots and 3 tablespoons water in a nonstick casserole. Cook over medium heat for about 2 minutes. Add the wine and bay leaf. Bring to a rapid boil, then lower the heat to medium-low and cook for 8–10 minutes.

2 Add the butter and mix well. Add the cayenne and salt and pepper, and mix again. Dissolve the cornstarch in the remaining table-spoon of water and add it to the wine. Continue to cook, stirring, for 1–2 minutes, until a sauce is formed. Remove the bay leaf before serving.

NOTE: This sauce is excellent over certain meat dishes, as well as over beans, especially red beans.

Onion Sauce

Makes 2 cups

2 ounces butter

4 medium onions, chopped finely

1 cup dry white wine or vermouth

Salt and freshly ground pepper

1/2 cup heavy cream

1 Melt the butter in a saucepan. Add the onions and sauté over medium heat for a few minutes. Add the wine and salt and pepper, and cook over low heat for 15–20 minutes, stirring from time to time. Add the heavy cream and mix thoroughly.

NOTE: This sauce can be used on eggs, potatoes, seafood, and certain meats.

Roquefort Sauce

1 Place the cheese, cream, butter, and wine in a nonstick saucepan. Heat over medium heat, stirring constantly, until a sauce is formed.

2 In a small bowl, dissolve the cornstarch in the stock and add to the sauce. Add pepper (and salt only if needed). Continue to stir for several minutes until a thicker consistency is achieved.

NOTE: This is an excellent sauce for certain vegetables, such as asparagus, broccoli, or cauliflower.

Makes 1 1/2 cups

2 ounces Roquefort cheese, crumbled

4 tablespoons heavy cream

2 tablespoons butter

1/2 cup dry white wine

1 tablespoon cornstarch

1/2 cup vegetable or chicken stock

Freshly ground pepper

Salt (optional)

Parsley Sauce

Pour the wine into a medium saucepan and add the shallots and bay leaf. Bring to a boil while stirring continuously. Add the stock and continue to cook, stirring, until it comes again to a boil. Lower the heat and continue to cook for 3 or 4 minutes, until the sauce is reduced to about $^3/4$ cup. At this point, add the cream and salt and pepper. Mix well and bring the sauce to another boil. Add the parsley and continue to cook, stirring, for another 5–6 minutes. Stir the sauce well and allow it to cool. When cool, puree the sauce in a blender, then return it to the saucepan and reheat it for a minute or two, stirring all the while. Serve hot.

NOTE: This sauce can be used in a variety of ways, over fish, vegetables, or egg dishes.

Makes 2 cups

$^1/_2$ cup white wine

6 shallots, minced

1 bay leaf

1 cup vegetable stock

$1^1/_2$ cup of heavy cream

Salt and freshly ground pepper

1 cup fresh parsley, minced or ground with
   a mortar and pestle

Crème Fraîche

Makes 2 cups

1 cup heavy cream (not ultrapasteurized)

1 cup dairy sour cream

Whisk heavy cream and sour cream together in a bowl. Cover loosely with plastic wrap and let sit in the kitchen or another warm place overnight, or until thickened. Cover and refrigerate for at least 4 hours. The crème fraîche will then be thick and ready to use. It will last for up to 2 weeks in the refrigerator.

Benedictine
Chutney Sauce

Makes about 1¹/2 cups

4 tablespoons olive oil

¹/2 pound ripe tomatoes, peeled, seeded, and
    chopped coarsely

1 large onion, chopped

3 cloves garlic, minced

¹/2 pound red apples, peeled, cored, and sliced

1 medium zucchini, cubed

1¹/2 cups cider vinegar

1 (1¹/2-ounce) package raisins

Brown or granulated sugar

Salt and freshly ground pepper

1 teaspoon ground cumin

A pinch grated nutmeg

1 teaspoon coriander seeds

1 Pour the oil into a large nonstick casserole and add all other ingredients. Simmer over low heat, stirring often, until the chutney becomes sauce-like and thick, 25–30 minutes. Check the seasonings, and when the chutney is done, turn off the heat and allow it to cool.

2 If the chutney is not going to be used immediately, pour it into a bowl and keep it in the refrigerator. Otherwise, sterilize some canning jars, pour the chutney into them, cover the jars, and place them into a bath of boiling water for 20 minutes, until the jars are thoroughly sealed.

NOTE: This chutney is a good accompaniment for lentil and rice dishes, as well as certain meats.

Simple Vinaigrette

Place the salt and pepper in a cup or bowl. Add the vinegar and stir thoroughly. Add the oil and stir until all the ingredients are completely blended.

Makes about 1 cup

1 teaspoon salt
1/2 teaspoon freshly ground pepper
3 tablespoons wine vinegar
6 tablespoons extra-virgin olive oil

Vinaigrette with Mustard

Prepare the Simple Vinaigrette as directed. Add 1 tablespoon of French mustard and whisk thoroughly.

Vinaigrette with Garlic

Prepare the Simple Vinaigrette as directed. Add 1 crushed, well minced garlic clove. Let the vinaigrette stand for a few hours before using.

Vinaigrette with Herbs

Prepare the Simple Vinaigrette as directed, but replace the vinegar with an equivalent amount of lemon juice. Add 1/4 cup of finely chopped mixed herbs (parsley, tarragon, chervil, and so on, as you prefer). Mix thoroughly.

Breads

he practice of bread making is as ancient as humanity itself. It has been here for thousands and thousands of years. History tells us that the ancient Egyptians invented the first ovens in their open fields for the sole purpose of baking their daily bread. The Greeks contributed their own talents to this ancient practice by discovering how to carefully mill and grind flour for baking. In the meantime, the old Romans—always avid bread consumers—updated the process of bread making in other ways and introduced their methods to the whole of the Roman empire. Throughout the centuries, monasteries developed their own traditions and particular recipes for making and baking bread. The monks created certain recipes for ordinary days, and others for more festive occasions such as Christmas, Epiphany, Easter, and Pentecost. Nothing is so appealing in the monastic kitchen as the fragrance of simple, fresh, baked bread. In the past, for years and years, I used to bake bread weekly, not only for consumption at the monastery, but also to sell at one of the local health food stores, where our fresh organic breads were deeply appreciated by the clientele.

There is no doubt in my mind that the making of delicious fresh bread is a cultivated art form. It demands time and patience to learn to do it properly. Obviously, the time preparation and the effort put into it bring their own rewards: quality of the bread, solid nutrition, and the pure delight that come from tasting such a good and authentic product, the fruit of our own labours! As James Beard is quoted as saying: "Good bread is the most fundamentally satisfying of all foods; and good bread with fresh butter is the greatest of all feasts."

Bread making using the inexpensive regular yeast one finds in the local supermarket is not necessarily a difficult task. And it doesn't consume endless amounts of time, either. A good baker must simply be careful in mixing the exact measures of ingredients, be patient in the kneading process and in the shaping of the loaves, and pay close attention to the rising and baking times so that the end result coincides exactly with what one had in mind from the beginning. There are hundreds and hundreds of recipes all around to choose from, for bread itself comes in many varieties, types, shapes, and sizes. The few recipes in this repertoire are some of the most used in our small monastic kitchen throughout the years. They are basic, simple, easy to prepare, and a pure delight to the palate. In my humble view, there is really nothing comparable to the allure of homemade bread. It feeds both the body and the soul!

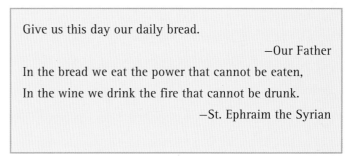

Give us this day our daily bread.

—Our Father

In the bread we eat the power that cannot be eaten,
In the wine we drink the fire that cannot be drunk.

—St. Ephraim the Syrian

Monastery Brioche

Makes 1 big loaf

1 ($\frac{1}{4}$-ounce) package active dry yeast

$\frac{1}{4}$ cup warm water

4 cups all-purpose flour

$\frac{1}{2}$ teaspoon salt

$\frac{1}{4}$ cup milk

2 tablespoons sugar

2 tablespoons honey

6 ounces butter, cut into small pieces, plus
    2 tablespoons, melted

6 eggs, beaten

1 In a small bowl, dissolve the yeast in the water. Pour the yeast mixture into a deep bowl and add 1 cup of the flour. Grease your hands with a bit of lard or butter, then mix the ingredients well by hand and shape into a ball. Cover with a damp kitchen towel and allow the dough to rise in a warm place for about 45 minutes.

2 Flour a board. Place the remaining 3 cups of flour in a large mixing bowl. Make a hollow well in the center of it and pour in the salt, milk, sugar, honey, eggs, and half of the cut butter. Work the mixture with your greased fingers, gradually mixing the flour with the other ingredients. When a dough is formed, place it on the floured board and knead it until the dough turns mellow and smooth. Punch it a couple of times to break up any air pockets.

3 Gradually add the remaining bits of butter to the dough, without necessarily kneading it in, simply mix the butter in. Add the risen ball of dough starter and gently knead it into the dough.

4 Again, shape the dough into a ball and place it in a greased bowl. Cover the bowl with a damp towel and let it stand at room temperature for several hours, until the dough has doubled in size. Punch down the dough and place it in the refrigerator for at least 4 hours or overnight.

5 Punch down the dough again and shape it into the shape of the pan to be used for baking, either a brioche mold, or loaf pan, or other shape. Generously butter the pan and place the dough into it, filling two-thirds of the pan. Cover with a damp towel and let the dough sit for 45 minutes or so, until it rises and again doubles in size. Midway through this period, preheat the oven to 400°F.

6 Brush the top of the dough with melted butter. With a small, sharp knife, gently make a cross in the center of the dough. Bake for 25–30 minutes, until the brioche has browned on the top or a thin knife inserted into the center comes out clean. Remove from the oven and allow to cool on a rack before serving.

Saint Anthony's Bread

Makes 2 loaves

1 (1/4-ounce) package active dry yeast

3 teaspoons sesame seeds

1 2/3 cups water

2 cups whole wheat flour

3 tablespoons chives, chopped finely

1 tablespoon salt

Cornmeal

1 Place the yeast and sesame seeds in a medium-size bowl. Stir in 1/2 cup of the water gradually until the yeast is dissolved. Continue gradually adding the remaining water.

2 Gradually add the flour, chives, and salt. Stir continually until a dough is formed.

3 Flour a board, place the dough on it, and knead gently for about 12 minutes. Place the dough in a large oiled bowl or casserole. Cover with a damp kitchen towel and allow the dough to rise in a warm place for about 1 hour, until it doubles in size.

4 After the dough rises, punch it down and knead once again for 6–8 minutes. Preheat the oven to 400°F. Sprinkle two large baking sheets with cornmeal. Divide the dough into two equal parts and shape them into round balls. Flatten them a bit at the center and place them on a baking sheet.

5 Cover the balls with damp towels and again let them rise until doubled in size, 30–45 minutes.

6 Bake the loaves for 40–45 minutes, until they turn brown and crispy on top. Allow the bread to cool on a rack before serving.

Saint Maur
Onion Bread

Makes 2 loaves

1 large onion, chopped finely, plus $^1/_3$ onion, chopped finely, for topping (optional)

$^1/_3$ cup olive oil

$^1/_2$ cup milk

4 tablespoons honey

2 teaspoons salt

1 cup water

1 ($^1/_4$-ounce) package active dry yeast

3 cups whole wheat flour

2 cups all-purpose flour

$^1/_2$ cup shredded cheddar cheese (optional)

1 Reserving the $^1/_3$ onion for an optional topping (if using), briefly sauté the onion in the olive oil in a nonstick saucepan over medium-low heat, until the onion begins to turn golden brown. Add the milk, honey, and salt, and stir until well blended. Continue to simmer the mixture over low heat.

2 In a separate saucepan, heat the water over low heat to lukewarm. Stir in the yeast. Turn off the heat and let the pan stand for about 5 minutes.

3 Flour a board. Pour the yeast mixture into a medium-size bowl. Add the onion mixture and stir gently. Grease your hands with a bit of lard or butter, then add the flour gradually, working it in by hand to form a dough. Knead the dough on the floured board for about 3 minutes.

4 Grease another large bowl or saucepan and place the dough in it. Cover it with a damp kitchen towel and allow the dough to rise in a warm place for about 1 hour, until it doubles in size.

5 Grease two 9 × 5 × 3-inch loaf pans. Punch down the dough and divide it into two equal portions. Knead again for 1 to 2 minutes and form two separate loaves. Place the loaves in the loaf pans. Cover them with a damp towel and let them rise again until they double in size, about 1–1$^1/_2$ hours. While the bread is rising, begin to preheat the oven to 350°F.

6 Bake for 30–35 minutes, until the tops turn brown and crispy. (Optional: During the last 5 minutes of baking, spread grated cheese on top of loaves and sprinkle with chopped onions.) Remove from the oven and allow to cool on a rack before serving.

Saint Placid
Whole Wheat Bread

Makes 2 loaves

3 cups whole wheat flour (stone-ground,
 if possible)

2¹/₂ teaspoons salt

2¹/₂ cups milk

¹/₄ cup molasses or honey

¹/₄ cup vegetable oil

2 (¹/₄-ounce) packages active dry yeast

1 egg, well beaten

¹/₂ cup all-purpose flour

¹/₂ cup wheat germ

1 Combine 2 cups of the whole wheat flour with the salt in a large mixing bowl.

2 Heat the milk over low heat to the point between lukewarm and warm. Add the molasses and vegetable oil. Stir until well blended. Turn off the heat and stir in the yeast. Let stand for 5 minutes.

3 Gradually add the milk mixture to the flour mixture, then stir in the beaten egg. Grease your hands with a bit of lard or butter, then add the remaining cup of whole wheat flour, the all-purpose flour, and the wheat germ, working it in by hand to form a dough. Sprinkle flour over a board, and gently knead the dough on the board for about 2 minutes, until it becomes soft and smooth.

4 Grease another large bowl or casserole and place the dough in it. Cover with a damp kitchen towel and allow the dough to rise in a warm place for about 1 hour, until it doubles in size.

5 Grease two 9 × 5 × 3-inch loaf pans. Punch down the dough and divide it into two equal portions. Knead each loaf again for 1 minute, and then place in the pans. Cover with a damp towel and let rise until again doubled in size. While the bread is rising, begin to preheat the oven to 350°F.

6 Bake for 40–45 minutes, until the loaves turn golden on the top and sound hollow when tapped. Remove the bread from the pans immediately and allow to cool on a rack before serving.

Avignon Banana and Raisin Bread

1 Preheat the oven to 350°F. In a large mixing bowl, beat the eggs lightly. Add the honey and vanilla and mix well.

2 Add the bananas to the egg mixture. Mix well.

3 In a separate bowl, mix the flour and baking powder together and stir gently, little by little, into the banana mixture. Add the raisins and stir to incorporate them.

4 Stir the butter into the mixture just until it is incorporated. Do not overmix the batter.

5 Generously butter a 9 × 5 × 3-inch loaf pan and pour the banana batter into it. Bake for 45–50 minutes. Insert a thin knife in the center; if it comes out clean, the bread is done. Remove from the oven and allow to cool a bit on a rack before turning out. Slice and serve.

Makes 1 loaf

2 eggs

6 tablespoons honey or maple syrup

1 tablespoon vanilla extract

4 medium bananas, well mashed

1¼ cups whole wheat flour

2 teaspoons baking powder

1 (1½-ounce) package raisins

5 tablespoons butter or margarine, melted

Laudate
Oatmeal Bread

Makes 2 loaves

2 cups water

$^3/_4$ cup margarine

2 (1 $^1/_2$-ounce) packages raisins

2 cups rolled oats

$^2/_3$ cup brown or granulated sugar

2 cups whole wheat flour

2 teaspoons baking powder

1 teaspoon baking soda

2 large eggs, beaten

1 Preheat the oven to 350°F.

2 Bring the water to a boil and add the margarine. Stir until it dissolves into the water. Turn off the heat. Add the raisins, oats, and sugar. Stir well and allow the mixture to stand until the oats absorb all the water.

3 In a deep bowl, mix together the flour, baking powder, and baking soda. Add the beaten eggs to the flour, and stir with a fork to mix well.

4 Add the oat mixture to the flour mixture, and with damp hands, knead the dough until it becomes uniform. Divide the dough into two equal portions.

5 Generously butter two 9 × 5 × 3-inch loaf pans and place the dough in them. Bake for 30–40 minutes, until the top begins to turn a deep brown. Insert a thin knife in the center; if it comes out clean, the bread is done. Remove from the oven and allow to cool on a rack before serving.

Part Five

Final Course

Fruits and Desserts

Fruits and Desserts

Desserts prepared and eaten in a monastery tend to express simplicity, straightforwardness, and just plain basic common sense. Very often, especially on weekdays and during Advent and Lent, our desserts consist foremost of fruits or some concoction made of fruits, such as compotes, baked apples, apple crisp, banana flambé, pears in wine, fruit salad, and so on. The same thing comes to pass when certain fruits are in season; they are presented often at the monastic table in one form or another. During the autumn harvest and the winter months, we eat apples in every form and combination available. Now and then, when a special feast day or other occasion arrives, we may prepare something more elaborate with them, or with pears or other fruits, such as a delicious, well-baked *tarte aux pommes*. These desserts, prepared only for special occasions or feast days, allow us to give in to small harmless indulgences that hopefully restore us not only physically but also spiritually. When we celebrate a particular feast day, or saint's day, or the onomastic of a monk (his name or patron saint's day), a good menu presented at the table, including a special dessert, it is an occasion for rejoicing, for giving thanks to God our provider, and for fraternal conviviality.

For Christmas, Easter, Thanksgiving, the Solemnities of the Lord, the feast day of the Mother of God, or Saint Benedict's Day, we may take the time in the monastic kitchen to prepare an unusual cake, tart, or pastry. This breaks the monotony of our everyday desserts and gives us all something to look forward to at the conclusion of a feast-day meal. Very often I may also prepare one the traditional French custards that we all grew up with, such as the now well-known crème caramel or some variation of the *crème pâtissière* or crème anglaise, as basis for other desserts. Certain creams, such as the famous Crème Chantilly, blend very well with fruits and other mixtures. I often turn to such creations as I find them well suited for retreat groups, families, or a monastic community. Although they are easy to pre-pare and rather informal in their presentation, they are always appreciated at the table. Some are even a bit entertaining, for monks are just as curious as anyone else, and they invariably wish to know where the recipe originated, from what country or monastery, or from what family member or chef. So much for the strange combination of virtue and monastic curiosity!

Many of the recipes presented here offer that same "home-made" feeling, that unique personal touch that makes some desserts so appetizing. It is true, for instance, that certain desserts demand time and thus are better left for weekends and days when one has more time. Baking a cake or scones may be a bit impractical during weekdays, especially for those who work outside the home; but on weekends and holidays nothing is more pleasing to the senses than a home-baked dessert. The aroma that rises from the oven alone is more than an incentive to gather around the kitchen and anticipate the joy of what one is going to taste. Baking is one of those ancient culinary traditions that deserves to be kept alive in every kitchen. These recipes, though simple and brief, offer the cook all sorts of assurances and flavors to please friends and family on any occasion.

> It's hard to beat an apple-something as one of America's favorite desserts . . . In the beginning, there was apple-sauce.
>
> —Julia Child, *The Way to Cook*

> Fruit and cream is a timeless combination. Whatever the particulars, the essence of fruit and cream seems to be found in the contrast of flavors and textures—the sweet, moist fruits paired with delicate, smoothly textured cream. Thick fresh cream is always delicious poured over fruit.
>
> —Deborah Madison, *The Savory Way*

Valence Chocolate Cake

Makes about 6–8 servings

12 tablespoons butter, cut into small pieces

8 ounces bittersweet chocolate, grated or
    finely chopped

4 tablespoons all-purpose flour

5 eggs, separated

1 cup sugar

1 recipe Crème Chantilly (page 241) (optional)

1 Preheat the oven to 350°F. Generously butter a 9-inch round Pyrex or ovenproof dish, and dust heavily with flour.

2 Melt the butter and chocolate in a bain-marie; that's to say, melt them together over medium-low heat in a medium bowl set over a large saucepan of lightly boiling water, stirring constantly with a sturdy wooden spoon. When melted and well blended, turn off the heat and remove the bowl from the saucepan Add the flour and egg yolks, and blend well with a mixer. Set the mixture aside and allow it to cool.

3 With a mixer, beat the egg whites in a large bowl for about 3 minutes, until firm and stiff. With the help of a spatula, fold one-quarter of the egg whites at a time into the flour mixture. Repeat until completely incorporated. Carefully pour the chocolate batter into the prepared baking dish.

4 Bake for about 30 minutes. Insert a toothpick into the center of the cake; if it comes out clean, the cake is done. Remove from the oven and allow to cool on a rack. Serve the cake at room temperature.

NOTE: On a special occasion or feast day, top the cake with Crème Chantilly, as they do in France.

Monaco Cherry Bread Pudding

Makes 8 servings

1 Preheat the oven to 300°F. Place the bread cubes on a baking sheet. Bake for about 12 minutes, until the bread is mildly toasted.

2 Place the cherries, pears, apples, and almonds in a casserole. Add the sherry and simmer gently over low heat for about 10 minutes, stirring from time to time, until most of the liquid evaporates. Remove from the heat. Cover and let stand until ready to be used.

3 In a very large bowl, whisk the milk, sugar, Calvados, and egg yolks. Gradually add the bread cubes and the fruit mixture. Mix all the ingredients well.

4 Beat the egg whites until stiff in a separate bowl and add about half of the whites to the fruit mixture. Fold in gently.

5 Butter an 11 × 7-inch baking dish. Pour the mixture into the dish and level the top. Spread the remaining egg whites over the top. Bake for 40–45 minutes. Remove from the oven. Allow the pudding to cool a bit on a rack before serving.

6 cups cubed whole wheat country-style bread

1 (16-ounce) can pitted black cherries, drained

2 medium pears, peeled and sliced into
    small pieces

2 medium red apples, peeled and sliced into
    small pieces

1 cup blanched almonds

1 cup sweet sherry

4 cups milk

½ cup sugar

2 teaspoons Calvados liqueur

5 eggs, separated

Henri IV Fig Compote

1 Pour the wine into a nonreactive saucepan. Add the sugar and bring to a rapid boil. Add the figs, raisins, cloves, and lemon juice, and lower the heat to medium-low.

2 Cook the figs for about 15 minutes, stirring from time to time. After 15 minutes, remove the figs and raisins and transfer them to a serving bowl or six individual dessert plates.

3 Continue to cook the wine mixture until it slowly turns into syrup. Turn off the heat, remove the cloves, allow the syrup to cool, and then pour it over the figs. Serve the compote lukewarm.

Makes 4–6 servings

3 cups sweet wine

3/4 cup brown or granulated sugar

1 pound dried figs, stemmed

1/2 cup dark raisins

5 whole cloves

1 tablespoon lemon juice

Acorn Squash Soufflé

Makes 6 servings

2 medium acorn squash
4 tablespoons unsalted butter
1/4 cup cornstarch
$1^1/_2$ cups milk
$^1/_4$ cup pure maple syrup
$^1/_2$ teaspoon salt
$^1/_2$ teaspoon ground cinnamon
A pinch grated nutmeg
2 teaspoons vanilla extract
5 egg, separated
$^1/_3$ cup sugar

1 Slice the squash in half, scoop out the seeds, and clean well the insides. Place the squash cut side down in a large pot filled with water. Add a pinch of salt and bring the water to a boil. Cook the squash for about 20 minutes. Drain and allow to cool.

2 With the help of a pointed spoon, scoop out the flesh into a bowl. Mash the squash thoroughly.

3 Melt the butter in a casserole over medium-low heat. Dissolve the cornstarch in the milk in a small bowl, and add gradually to the melted butter while stirring continually. Add the maple syrup, salt, cinnamon, nutmeg, and vanilla. Continue to stir until the mixture is well blended and begins to thicken. Remove from the heat.

4 Preheat the oven to 350°F and butter a large soufflé dish. In a large bowl, beat the egg yolks with a mixer. Gradually add the squash, the cornstarch mixture, and the sugar. Continue to beat with the mixer until the mixture becomes smooth and well blended

5 In a separate bowl, beat the egg whites stiff with clean beaters. Fold about $^1/_2$ cup of the stiffened egg whites into the squash mixture. Pour this mixture into the prepared soufflé dish. With the help of a spatula, fold the remaining egg whites into the mixture. Bake for about 45 minutes. Serve hot.

NOTE: This is a lovely dessert to serve throughout the cold winter months and on special occasions, such as Thanksgiving and other festive winter days.

Clafouti with Seedless Grapes

Makes 6–8 servings

2 cups whole milk

4 eggs

$^1/_3$ cup all-purpose or whole wheat flour

$^1/_2$ cup granulated sugar

2 teaspoons vanilla extract

A pinch salt

2 pounds white seedless grapes, stemmed,
   well washed, and dried

Confectioners' sugar (optional)

1 Preheat the oven to 350°F.

2 Place in a blender the milk, eggs, flour, granulated sugar, vanilla, and salt. Whirl until the mixture is smooth. Set aside.

3 Generously butter an 8 × 8-inch ovenproof dish. (It should be at least 2 inches deep.) Pour about one-quarter of the batter into the dish and place it in the oven for 3–4 minutes, until the batter sets at the bottom of the dish. Carefully remove the dish from the oven and distribute the individual grapes evenly over the entire surface of the batter. (Optional: Sprinkle some granulated sugar over the grapes.) Again, with great care, pour the rest of the batter over the grapes, to cover them completely.

4 Place the dish in the center of the oven and bake for 25–30 minutes. The clafouti is done when the top puffs and turns lightly brown yet the consistency remains custardlike.

5 Remove from the oven, sprinkle with confectioners' sugar, and serve while the caflouti is warm.

1 Wash and drain the fruit. Set it aside.

2 Place the egg yolks in a deep nonreactive metal bowl. Add the granulated sugar and vermouth.

3 Place the bowl over a pot of simmering water and whip the egg mixture with a mixer until it reaches a thick consistency. Refrigerate for about 2 hours.

4 In a separate bowl, place the heavy cream, confectioners' sugar, and vanilla. Whip until stiff. Mix half of this with the egg yolk mixture, and set the other half aside to be used for garnish.

5 Divide the fruit among six glass bowls or serving dishes. Pour the sauce evenly over the fruit. Top each serving with the rest of the whipped cream. Chill in the refrigerator and serve cold.

Saint Peter's
Zabaglione

Makes 6 servings

1 pint raspberries

1 pint strawberries

6 egg yolks

$3/4$ cup granulated sugar

$3/4$ cup good-quality sweet vermouth

$3/4$ cup heavy cream

$1/2$ cup confectioners' sugar

A dash vanilla extract

Country Compote

Makes 6–8 servings

1 butternut squash, peeled, seeded, and cubed

4 red apples, peeled, cored, and sliced
    into quarters

$1/2$ pound dried prunes, pitted and halved

4 teaspoons cloves

$1/2/$ cup sugar

Zest of 1 lemon, grated

1 teaspoon ground cinnamon

3 tablespoons Calvados or other apple or
    pear liqueur

1 Place the squash cubes in a large saucepan, add about 4 cups of water, and bring to a boil. Lower the heat to medium, cover, and cook for about 15 minutes, until tender.

2 Add the apples, prunes, cloves, sugar, lemon zest, cinnamon, and liqueur. Re-cover the saucepan and continue to cook for another 15 minutes, stirring occasionally.

3 When the compote is done, remove the lemon zest and check the seasonings. Allow the compote to cool and then place it in the refrigerator to chill for several hours before serving. Serve cold.

1 Place the rice in a saucepan, add 4 cups of water, and bring to a boil; cook for 5 minutes, then drain.

2 Pour 3 cups of the milk into a nonstick saucepan and add the rice, half the vanilla bean, and $^{1}/_{2}$ cup of the granulated sugar. Cook over medium-low heat until the rice is cooked and has thickened, 20–30 minutes. Toward the end of the cooking, add the raisins and mix well.

3 Beat the egg yolks with the remaining $^{1}/_{2}$ cup of granulated sugar in a double boiler. Beat until the mixture becomes smooth and creamy. Heat the remaining 3 cups of milk in a separate pan, and when hot, pour it gradually into the egg mixture, adding also the other half of the vanilla bean. Continue to cook over medium-low heat, stirring continually, until the custard thickens. Add a pinch of cinnamon and the grated lemon zest. Mix well and remove the vanilla beans. Turn off the heat and allow the custard to cool.

4 To make the Crème Chantilly, in a deep bowl, whip the cream and confectioner's sugar with the help of a mixer until frothy. Fold gradually into the custard. Chill for several hours. Just before serving, sprinkle some ground cinnamon on top.

Empress Eugenie
Rice Pudding

Makes 4–6 servings

$^{2}/_{3}$ cup uncooked white rice

6 cups milk

1 vanilla bean, cut into 2 pieces

1 cup granulated sugar

$^{1}/_{2}$ cup raisins

6 egg yolks

A pinch cinnamon, plus additional for garnish

Zest of 1 lemon, finely grated

Crème Chantilly:

1 cup heavy cream

$^{1}/_{3}$ cup confectioners' sugar

Baked Anjou Pears

Makes 4 servings

4 Anjou pears, peeled and sliced into
    perfect halves
8 teaspoons maple syrup
Brown or granulated sugar
4 tablespoons butter, cut into small pieces
$1/2$ cup heavy cream
4 egg whites

1 Preheat the oven to 350°F and thoroughly butter an 11 × 7-inch ovenproof dish.

2 Carefully scoop out with a sharp knife the seeds at the core of the fruit. Arrange the pears on the baking dish, closely packed against each other.

3 Pour 1 teaspoon of the maple syrup over each pear half at the center and let it run over. Sprinkle the brown sugar over the surface of the pears. Distribute the butter over the pears. Bake for about 20 minutes.

4 In a large bowl, beat the egg whites with a mixer until stiff. Pour the cream evenly over all the pears and, with a spatula, spread the egg whites on top of the cream. Place the dish back in the oven and bake for another 10 minutes or so, until the egg whites brown. Serve warm.

Dauphin Easy Apple Soufflé

Makes 4–6 servings

4 Golden Delicious apples, peeled, cored, and sliced

¾ cup sugar

½ teaspoon ground cinnamon

3 eggs, separated

1½ cups milk

½ cup all-purpose flour

½ teaspoon baking powder

3 tablespoons Calvados liqueur

1 Preheat the oven to 350°F. Generously butter an 11 × 7-inch baking dish. Arrange the apple slices neatly in the dish. Sprinkle with ¼ cup of sugar and sprinkle the cinnamon over the apples.

2 Place the egg yolks in a blender, add the milk, and whirl thoroughly. Add the remaining ½ cup sugar, milk, flour, baking powder, and liqueur and whirl some more until well blended. Cover the top of the apples with the mixture.

3 In a large bowl, beat the egg whites stiff with a mixer and, with a spatula, spread it over the entire top of the egg yolk mixture. Bake for 35–40 minutes. Remove from the oven and serve hot.

Chambord Zabaglione

1 Whisk the egg yolks, Chambord, and sugar in medium metal bowl. Set the bowl over saucepan of simmering water. Whisk the mixture constantly and vigorously until thickened and an instant-read thermometer inserted into the mixture registers 140°F for 3 minutes, about 5 minutes total.

2 Remove the bowl from the saucepan. Add the cream and whisk until incorporated. Serve warm or chilled.

Makes about $1^2/3$ cups

6 large egg yolks

$1/3$ cup Chambord or other liqueur

3 tablespoons superfine or granulated sugar

$1/4$ cup heavy cream

Buttermilk Panna Cotta

1 Soften the gelatin in the cold water in a medium bowl for about 5 minutes. Meanwhile, combine the cream and sugar in a small saucepan. Scrape the seeds from the vanilla pod into the pan, then add the pod. Heat the cream over medium heat, stirring until the sugar dissolves, 3–5 minutes, then stir into the bowl of gelatin. Stir in the buttermilk, then strain into another bowl.

2 Divide custard among six 8-ounce ramekins and refrigerate until set, about 3 hours. To unmold, dip the ramekins into a dish of hot water, then invert the custards onto plates. Garnish with raspberries or other fruit, if you like.

Makes 6 servings

$1^1/2$ teaspoons unflavored gelatin

1 tablespoon cold water

$1^1/4$ cups heavy cream

7 tablespoons sugar

$1/2$ vanilla pod, split lengthwise

$1^3/4$ cups buttermilk

Raspberries or other fruit (optional)

Raspberry Mousse

1 Refrigerate a large bowl to chill it. Place the raspberries and the granulated sugar in a separate bowl and toss to mix. Let stand for 20 minutes.

2 Place half of the raspberries in a food processor or blender. With a large, sharp knife, finely chop the remaining raspberries. Puree the removed berries and return them to the chopped berries.

3 Whip the cream, confectioners' sugar, and crème de cassis in the chilled bowl, until stiff. Gradually fold the raspberry mixture into the cream mixture. Mix well and refrigerate for at least 3 hours before serving. Garnish the top with mint leaves, if desired.

Makes 4 servings

1 pint raspberries, washed and trimmed

$1/4$ cup granulated sugar

$1 1/2$ pints heavy cream

$1/3$ cup confectioners' sugar

4 teaspoons crème de cassis

Fresh mint leaves, for garnish (optional)

Rustic Omelet with Fruit

Makes 4 servings

2 large apples, peeled, cored, and sliced

3 pears, peeled, cored, and sliced

7 tablespoons granulated sugar

5 tablespoons Calvados liqueur

6 eggs, separated

A pinch salt

4 tablespoons unsalted butter

Confectioners' sugar

1 Place the sliced fruit in a deep bowl and add 4 tablespoons of the granulated sugar and 3 tablespoons of the Calvados. Toss gently and let stand for 1 hour.

2 Preheat the oven to 375°F.

3 Place the egg yolks in another deep bowl and add the remaining 3 tablespoons of granulated sugar and the remaining 2 tablespoons of Calvados. Beat with an electric mixer until thick and smooth. Place the egg whites in a separate bowl, add a pinch of salt, and beat with the electric mixer until stiff and foamy. Gently fold, in small amounts at a time, into the egg yolk mixture.

4 Just before serving, melt the butter in a large cast-iron or ovenproof skillet. Pour in the egg mixture and spread it evenly over the whole skillet, smoothing the top. Cook over medium heat. When the omelet begins to rise, evenly spread the fruit over the entire top. Transfer the skillet to the oven and bake for 6–7 minutes, until the top turns golden brown. Dust the top of the omelet with confectioners' sugar, and serve hot. (This dessert should always be served hot.)

Natas

Makes 4–6 servings

1 cup heavy cream

2 teaspoons cornstarch

1 cup milk

5 egg yolks

$2/3$ cup sugar

2 teaspoons orange flower or vanilla extract

Ground cinnamon

1 Pour the cream into the top of a double boiler, set over a bottom filled partway with water. Dissolve the cornstarch in the milk in a small bowl, and add to the cream. In a deep bowl, beat the egg yolks and sugar with a mixer and add to the cream mixture. Add the orange flower extract.

2 Heat the double boiler over medium heat; when the water begins to boil, lower the heat to medium-low. Stir the cream continuously until it comes to a boil and thickens. Taste and add more sugar if necessary. When the cream is perfectly smooth and of an even consistency, remove it from the heat and pour into four to six small ramekins. Sprinkle with cinnamon and place in the refrigerator for several hours to chill before serving.

NOTE: This Portuguese dessert comes from an old monastery of nuns.

Jacob's Pear Flan

Makes 4–6 servings

1 Preheat the oven to 350°F. Place the flour, granulated sugar, and yeast in a deep bowl and mix well. Mix the egg yolks, milk, and vanilla together in a separate bowl and add to the flour mixture. Beat well with a mixer.

2 Melt the butter in a saucepan and add to the mixture. Again use a mixer to beat the ingredients well.

3 In another bowl, using clean beaters, beat the egg whites until stiff. Gradually fold them into the flour mixture.

4 Generously butter an 11 × 7-inch ovenproof dish and pour the mixture into it. Distribute the sliced pears over the entire top surface. Bake for 35–40 minutes. Just before serving, sprinkle confectioners' sugar on top. Serve the flan warm or at room temperature.

$^1/_2$ cup all-purpose flour

$^3/_4$ cup granulated sugar

1 ($^1/_4$-ounce) package active dry yeast

3 eggs, separated

2 cups milk

4 tablespoons ($^1/_2$ stick) butter

$^1/_2$ pound pears, peeled, cored, and sliced thinly

2 teaspoons vanilla extract

Confectioners' sugar

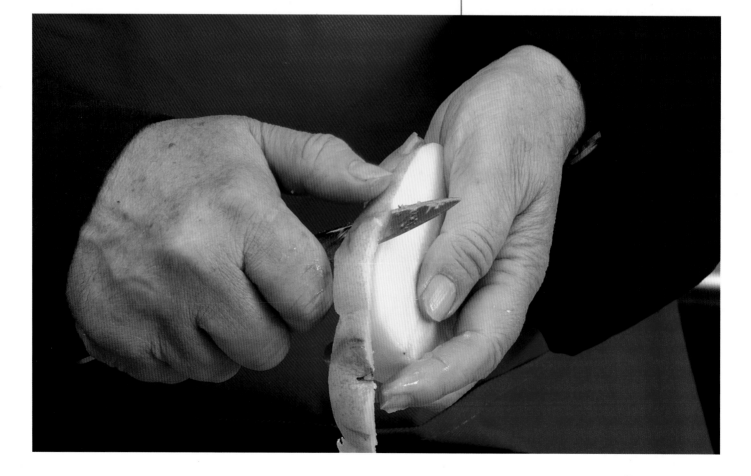

Tapioca and Strawberry Parfait

1 In a medium saucepan combine the milk, eggs, orange liqueur, tapioca, and half of the sugar. Blend well with a mixer or whisk by hand. Let stand for 5 or 6 minutes. Then, over medium heat, bring the tapioca mixture to a rolling boil, stirring continually. Remove the saucepan from the heat, add the vanilla, and stir well. Allow the tapoica mixture to cool for about 30 minutes.

2 Place the crushed strawberries in a food processor and pulse for a few short bursts until they reach a creamy consistency. Pour the strawberries into a separate saucepan, add the rest of the sugar, and cook for a few minutes over medium-low heat until well blended. Transfer to a medium bowl and set into a larger bowl of ice and cold water. Allow the strawberry mixture to cool, stirring from time to time, until it turns cold and frosty.

3 Transfer the tapioca mixture to a separate medium bowl and set into a larger bowl of ice and cold water. Allow the tapioca mixture to cool, stirring from time to time, until it turns cold and frosty.

4 Choose the serving glasses for the parfait. They should be at least 5 or 6 inches tall. Fill the glasses: First 2 tablespoons of the strawberry mixture followed by 2 tablespoons of the tapioca mixture, then continue alternating the mixtures, ending with the tapioca mixture on the top. Refrigerate and keep the parfaits chilled until ready to serve. Garnish each parfait with a fresh strawberry.

Makes 4–6 servings

3$\frac{1}{2}$ cups whole milk

2 medium eggs

1 tablespoon orange liqueur

4$\frac{1}{2}$ teaspoons quick-cooking tapioca

$\frac{1}{2}$ cup sugar

$\frac{1}{2}$ teaspoon vanilla extract

1 cup strawberries, cleaned and hulled, lightly crushed with a large knife, plus 4–6 whole berries, for garnish

1 Preheat the oven to 350°F. Place the milk, eggs, sugar, and peach liqueur in a blender and blend at high speed for about 2 minutes.

2 Generously butter an 8 × 8-inch baking dish about 2 inches deep. Pour about one-quarter of the batter into the baking dish and place the dish in the oven for about 3 minutes, until the batter has set in the bottom of the dish.

3 Remove the dish from the oven and arrange the peach halves evenly over the batter, sliced side down. Pour the rest of the batter on over the peaches and all around them. Bake for 35–40 minutes. The clafouti is done when the top begins to puff and turn brown, while the consistency remains custardlike. Remove the dish from the oven and sprinkle confectioners' sugar on top. Serve the clafouti warm.

NOTE: If pressed for time, you may use canned peach halves for the clafouti. If that is the case, be sure to drain them thoroughly of their juice.

Peach Clafouti

Makes 6 servings

1 1/2 cups milk

4 eggs

1/2 cup granulated sugar

3 tablespoons peach liqueur or vanilla extract

6 peaches, peeled, pitted, and sliced into
    perfect halves

Confectioners' sugar

Saint Scholastica
Peach Torte

1 Preheat the oven to 250°F. Prepare the pastry shell: Place all the pastry shell ingredients in a deep bowl and use a fork and damp hands to mix until a dough forms. Do not overmix the dough. Shape into a ball and place in the refrigerator for at least 1 hour.

2 Sprinkle flour over a flat surface and carefully roll out the dough, extending it in every direction. Sprinkle a bit of flour on top as you roll the dough. Generously butter a tart dish and carefully place the rolled dough in it. Trim the edges, forming some sort of decorative design. Cover the pastry shell with foil and prebake in the oven for about 12 minutes.

3 Prepare the custard: Blend all the custard ingredients in a bowl with an electric mixer or by hand. Pour the mixture into the prebaked pastry shell and place back into the oven for another 8–10 minutes, until the filling sets. Remove from the oven.

4 Place the peach slices over the set custard, following the design of a revolving wheel.

5 Prepare the topping: In a small nonstick saucepan, melt the peach jam and add the liqueur, water, and sugar. Stir until well blended. Carefully pour over the peaches and spread evenly with a brush.

6 Raise the oven temperature to 350°F. Bake the tart for about 30 minutes. (If the pastry browns too much, cover it with foil.) Remove from the oven and allow to cool on a rack before serving.

Makes 6 servings

Pastry shell:

1 egg

1/2 cup all-purpose flour

1/2 cup whole wheat flour

8 tablespoons (1 stick) butter, cut into pieces

5 tablespoons ice water

A pinch salt

2 teaspoons sugar

Custard:

2 egg yolks

4 tablespoons sugar

1/2 cup half-and-half

1 tablespoon peach liqueur

Filling:

6 peaches, peeled, pitted, and sliced

2 tablespoons lemon juice

1/3 cup sugar

Topping:

4 tablespoons peach jam

2 tablespoons peach liqueur

1 tablespoon water

1 teaspoon sugar

Apricots
Flambé

Makes 6 servings

2 cups water

1/2 cup sugar

3 teaspoons dried lavender buds (be sure to use culinary-grade lavender)

2 tablespoons apricot or peach liqueur

12 apricots, peeled, pitted, and sliced into perfect halves

1/2 cup dark rum

1 cup heavy cream or vanilla ice cream

1 Place the water in a casserole. Add the sugar, lavender, and liqueur, and bring to a rapid boil. Lower the heat to low, cover, and continue to cook for another 20 minutes, until a syrup is formed.

2 Add the apricots to the syrup and continue to cook over low heat for 12–15 minutes, always covered. Remove the apricots and set them aside for a few minutes to drain properly.

3 Just before serving, place the apricots in a large nonstick skillet, pour the rum evenly over them, raise the heat to medium, and with a match carefully light the rum. When the flame disappears, the flambé process is done. Serve four slices per person, and add a touch of cream or ice cream on top.

Melon with Strawberry and Raspberry

1 Combine the berries in a large dish and sprinkle with granulated sugar.

2 In a bowl, mix the vermouth and lemon juice and pour over the fruit. Place the dish in the refrigerator at least 2 hours before serving.

3 Prepare the sauce: Place the yogurt in a deep bowl. Add the confectioners' sugar and crème de cassis. Beat well with an electric mixer and refrigerate until ready to be served.

4 Divide the melon slices among four to six serving dishes. In each dish, form a six-pointed star with them, leaving space between, and place the berries between the slices. Place a big scoop of yogurt sauce at the center of the star and serve.

Makes 4–6 servings

$^1/_4$ pound strawberries, washed and hulled

$^1/_4$ pound raspberries, washed and trimmed

$^1/_2$ cup granulated sugar

$^1/_2$ cup sweet red vermouth

2 tablespoons lemon juice

2 small, ripe melons, peeled, seeded, and cut lengthwise into enough slices to provide each portion with six slices

Sauce:

1 (12-ounce) container low-fat plain yogurt

$^1/_2$ cup confectioners' sugar, or more if desired

3 tablespoons crème de cassis

Index